INDEX OF LEADING SPIRITUAL INDICATORS

GEORGE BARNA

INDEX

of LEADING

SPIRITUAL

INDICATORS

WORD PUBLISHING

DALLAS LONDON VANCOUVER MELBOURNE

WORD PUBLISHING
1996

Book design by Mark McGarry
Set in Minion & Syntax

LIBRARY OF CONGRESS CATALOGING-IN-PUBLICATION DATA:
Barna, George.
Index of leading spiritual indicators / George Barna.
p. cm.
Includes bibliographical references and index.
ISBN 0-8499-3603-9
1. United States—Religion—1960.
2. Public opinion—United States. I. Title.
BL2525.B38 1996 95-52904
200'.973'09049—dc20 95-52904
CIP

Printed in the United States of America

67890 QBP 54321

CONTENTS

INTRODUCTION

Rule Number One of American culture is "things change." Perhaps that rule should be amended to read "things change—quickly, unpredictably, and inconsistently."

New evidence of this truth emerges every day. In fact, without much difficulty you could probably identify a handful of organizations, processes, services, and products which we dismissed as absurd, faddish, irrelevant, or destined to failure just a few years ago, but which are the standard-bearers of the new America. In our haste to get on the bandwagon of the "new paradigm," we forget (or, in some cases, deny) the ridicule we heaped upon these groundbreakers just a few years earlier.

The common thread that joins the current crop of resuscitated pioneers is the speed and simplicity of their product and how it is delivered to the consumer. *USA Today*, initially derided as "McNews," has succeeded in redefining journalism that satisfies the masses. "CNN Headline News," initially berated by the critics as a throw-away cable service, has fundamentally reshaped how television communicates world events. No-frills options, such as those available from renegade airlines like Southwest or warehouse retailers like Sam's Club, meet the needs of millions of consumers. Consumer-sensitive, entrepreneurial upstarts, offering services ranging from fast food to the simplest of software applications routinely steal away market share from venerable industry giants. Their secret? Not superior product quality but accessibility, value, convenience, and ease of use—a very different set of needs to meet than existed just twenty years ago.

Recent developments within our culture have given birth to

many paradoxes. Our attention has become more narrowly focused even though our options proliferate. We demand that products become simpler in an environment of increasing complexity and heightened expectations. Household incomes and disposable revenue have been declining for six years, but we guard our time more fervently than our money regardless. At the same time that society demands greater quantities of information and increased interactivity, decisions are expected to happen more rapidly than ever.

And then there's religion.

Even the religious frontier has undergone dramatic changes in the past quarter century. A domain once thought to be impervious to the ravages and whims of societal transformations, religion at the end of the millennium is experiencing upheavals of gargantuan proportions. Yet, in the midst of the information explosion and a media that meddles in every arena of endeavor known to humankind, surprisingly little is known about the true nature of the shifts that are redirecting the religious frontier in America. The reality of the spiritual realm has remained inexplicably hidden from the masses in spite of widespread interest in religious matters.

While developing this book, I have only half-kiddingly thought of it as a kind of *Cliff Notes Guide to Spirituality— McFaith*, if you will. No matter how intrigued people are by the faith frontier, most adults just don't have the time—or won't *make* the time—to wade through tomes crammed with ponderous arguments or enlightening statistics, no matter how compelling the topic. In our mile-a-minute culture, we want the heart of the argument spelled out in elementary and precise terms—and with pictures, whenever possible. It's not that Americans can't think or won't think. We've simply discovered that if we hold out long enough, someone will distill a subject down to the few kernels of insight that we need or want. That is the outgrowth of a capitalistic system.

A poignant example of the fact that we live in a give-me-the-facts-fast-and-simple culture is the publication and immediate acceptance of William Bennett's brief book, *The Index of Leading Cultural Indicators*. In a scant 105 pages of liberally-spaced content, with ample charts and graphs to illustrate his points, Bennett made a provocative, yet non-combative, inoffensive portrait of the cultural demise of the nation. He focused on just a handful of elements—crime, family and children, youth behavior, education, pop culture, and religion—to arrive at a surprisingly comprehensive overview of where the nation was years earlier and where it is today. Through an artful, if sparse, blend of statistics, commentary, quotes, and graphics, Bennett documented what he termed the "substantial social regression" of America since the sixties.

The Index of Leading Cultural Indicators is noteworthy for several reasons. First, it re-ignited the endless debate between conservatives and liberals regarding the state of our society and the appropriate policy directions and solutions to pursue.

Second, and more importantly, it represents perhaps the first time that the population-at-large has at its disposal a range of reliable statistical data, narrowed down to the essence of objective sociological perspective. Bennett's screening of the available wealth of data down to a manageable portfolio of pieces of knowledge has enabled untrained individuals to make sense out of the current societal malaise. At last, thanks to Bennett's yeoman efforts, anyone and everyone may benefit from research data which, adeptly handled, tell a powerful story of cultural dissipation.

3

Third, and probably most importantly, Bennett tied religious faith to cultural health. While this correlation did not endear Bennett to the guardians of the "conventional wisdom"— i.e., that religion is a separate, insignificant, and ineffectual component of American life—the inclusion of religion as a core element in the modern malaise represents an honest attempt to identify and understand one of the key factors behind the steady collapse of a society which gives the outer appearance of strength, stability, and success. Bennett's numbers suggest that we are a nation rotting from the inside out.

If I were to level a criticism toward Bennett's wonderful book, though, it would be the inadequate treatment given to spiritual matters. His book would have been enhanced by incorporating more religious measures into his mix of key factors, for spirituality is indisputably a central facet of the American experience and related to the dilemma in which our nation finds itself today. The failure to understand the role of spirituality in our culture renders a social analyst incapable of completely comprehending the dynamics of American life. Because spiritual reality informs all other aspects of our lives, attempting to reach conclusions about life in the United States without a serious examination of religious perspectives and behaviors is an indication of either professional immaturity or personal prejudice—neither of which is tenable.

So the information in this book represents the missing link, as it were—a means to getting a grip on the spiritual dimension of America. Please realize that producing this resource goes beyond one man's personal desire to raise the public's consciousness of the importance of religion in life. Apparently, such a consciousness already exists, if we observe the degree of attention

Americans focus upon religious realities and considerations. Take note of some of the evidence.

- During the past five years, the bestseller lists have been sprinkled with books relating to angels, life after death, the spiritual principles of worldly success, the search for meaning through spiritual discovery, and other titles which have popularized spirituality.

- Candidates for public office, from the presidency down to mayor, regularly invoke the name of God, as if to hint that they are intimate with the ultimate powers that be. Far from being outraged by such vapid allusions to faith, the electorate expects such statements of spiritual sensitivity.

- Government officials frequently position policy changes in light of the importance of creating an environment for positive values and morality.

- Entertainers ranging from rock stars, TV celebrities, and movie icons to professional athletes and novelists publicly and proudly proclaim their spirituality. Some religious groups have even taken to actively pursuing endorsements from high-profile entertainers as a means of attracting attention and, hopefully, new adherents.

- Theological seminaries are experiencing an explosion of applications from people in their thirties and forties as Baby Boomers shift from a focus on achievement to a desire for significance, leaving promising secular careers for a life of piety and downward mobility.

- Medical and psychological researchers regularly release findings from their studies which underscore the benefits and advantages of religiosity. While such studies often create a professional uproar, the basis of the challenges to those studies tends to be emotional rather than scientific.

- Pop culture, once enamored by Nietszche's claim that "God is dead," has deemed things spiritual to be fashionable. Various forms of deity and spiritual beings have become a common focus in song lyrics, visual images (e.g., videos), and philosophical reflections. Rather than proclaim God to be dead, god (the abiblical, small "g" variety of deity) is now a multifarious entity which continues to fascinate each new generation in a novel way. Movies, MTV, on-line computer services, and even the broadcast networks frequently indulge in the consideration of spiritual matters.

- Public-opinion polls verify the nation's obsession with religion by consistently reporting high and sometimes surging levels of public interest in religion. Similarly, studies which measure lifestyle patterns would be incomplete without the inclusion of people's religious experience.

- Involvement with religious organizations—churches, synagogues, spiritual centers—continues to hold its own in the face of intense competition for people's time. People give more money to religious organizations than to any other realm of charitable or public service endeavor. Americans donate more hours of volunteer time to religious causes than to any other type of activity. And most adults claim some type of allegiance to a faith group.

- Religious media continue to enjoy enormous, if barely publicized, popularity. Tens of millions of Americans watch religious TV programming every month. Christian radio programs are even more widely absorbed by the public. Religious book sales are climbing every year. Christian music has passed several other categories, such as jazz and classical, in sales volume.

No, it doesn't take The Amazing Kreskin to discern that Americans are intrigued by and involved with religion. In many ways, the religious landscape is as broad as the nation's geography: the beliefs and religious practices of the people are as diverse and extensive as the nation's terrain. In fact, some contend that the scope of American theology and practice are as inclusive as anywhere on the planet. But such variety of belief and practice upholds rather than negates the reality that faith is a core component of the American experience.

The spiritual landscape of America in the twenty-first century is radically different from that of the forefathers of the nation. Yet, it is the openness to individualized expressions of faith which indicates the maturing of the American experiment in democracy. Indeed, the emphasis upon spiritual matters is by design rather than by chance. Historian Will Durant once noted that "the soul of a civilization is its religion." America, now well into its third century, is a country actively cultivating its soul.

The spirituality of the U.S. is not a recent response to modernism, materialism, communism, or any other worldly contrivance. The pilgrims made their journey to American soil in search of opportunities to worship their God in ways which were true to their beliefs. The founding fathers of the nation went to great lengths to protect variety in religious expression as well as the right to pursue religious faith whenever and however a person was so moved.

In 1831, impressed by America's unique and apparently successful justice system, a respected French magistrate journeyed across the Atlantic to study the American penal system. Upon examining the workings of the judicial and penal processes, however, Alexis de Tocqueville determined that the system could not be understood outside of its unique cultural context. In his renowned description of the reasons underlying America's success, Tocqueville argued that the American form of democracy was partially viable because of the spiritual commitment of the populace. Remove the freedom to pursue one's faith of choice—or the widespread inclination to deploy that freedom—and the nation would have long since deteriorated into anarchy, a country of individuals dedicated to turning equality into little more than the bold pursuit of personal well-being.

Today, the U.S. is home to many co-existing religious cultures and spiritual subgroups. But just how spiritually diverse are we? Is our faith, as some claim, "a mile wide and an inch deep?" How significant is religious faith in the turbulent mix of contemporary lifestyles? Does God matter to Americans—and, if so, *which* god? Journalists offer an endless stream of anecdotal evidence to suggest that there is no longer a spiritual consensus in the nation. Are they correct? On what basis are such claims of spiritual diversity made?

This book takes a step toward answering such questions. Based on survey research spanning the eighties and nineties, I will endeavor to provide a broad perspective regarding the contemporary spiritual condition of America just before we set foot into the third millennium. This is the story of a religious people and how they express their religious lives—personally, corporately, and culturally.

The objective of this book is to provide an accessible, broadbased assessment of the religious condition of America at the end of the twentieth century. In the interest of providing a relatively objective evaluation, the focus is upon "what" rather than "why." *What* do we believe? *What* do we do related to religious faith? *What* is the role of religion in our lives?

The information displayed in these pages is from nationwide surveys conducted by the Barna Research Group, Ltd. between 1982 and 1996, more than a decade's-worth of public opinion and behavioral information related to religious matters. The information has been divided into fourteen chapters, each devoted to a unique aspect of religious reality. Chapter 13 differs from its predecessors in that it provides several indices developed to integrate the wealth of data into a few summary measures of spirituality. Like any sociological measure, they are imperfect tools, but they may be helpful in discovering patterns or trends. And, like any sociologist with a teacher's heart, I could not resist the opportunity to provide at least a brief interpretation of what it all means. Since there are brief commentaries throughout the book offering subjective views of the information from myself as well as a host of other religious and social analysts, Chapter 14 represents a final word intended to provide the "big picture" on how all these data fit together and what they say about our religious lives—indeed, about our character overall.

For a book that purports to provide an objective view of America's religious reality, you may be surprised that so much attention is devoted to the Christian faith. This is not by accident, but neither is it by personal prejudice. My rationale—and I do believe it is that, not merely a rationalization—is that America is certainly a *culturally* diverse nation, but it is not as *religiously* diverse as some believe (or desire). Focusing so extensively upon Christianity as the present-day spiritual preference of America may not be politically correct, but it is sociologically defensible. As you peruse the information provided in these pages, you will discover that while traditional—some would say "biblical"— Christianity is certainly on the decline, most Americans continue to think of themselves as Christian individuals residing within a Christian nation. The concept of a "post-Christian" culture has merit, but most people continue to think of themselves as Christian in theology and in practice.

One of the exhilarating challenges, then, is to define the form and substance of modern American religion and compare it to the biblical model from which it ostensibly originates. The information contained in this volume should help make sense of what are—now—two disparate forms of religious perception and expression.

Even though I have offered brief overviews of the data in each section, and a more extensive personal interpretation of the facts in the closing chapter, this intentionally slim volume provides you with the same information from which my analysis was conceived, enabling you to examine the raw information toward developing your own speculations and conclusions. I am quite confident you will agree that Americans are *religious* people. Personally, I am less persuaded that we are truly a *Christian* people, regardless of our self-perceptions. But that is just one of the interpretations I have offered which you may accept or reject, based on the data provided in these pages.

America's religious perspective, like its cultural context, is constantly and rapidly changing. However, we stubbornly refuse to give up on the significance of personal and corporate spirituality. And that, perhaps as much as any other indicator, suggests that America retains the raw material of a nation with the potential to become moral, ethical, values-driven—in short, a healthy and esteemable society.

BEFORE YOU BEGIN

To help you understand and use the data to follow, the number preceding the description of the research study conducted by the Barna Research Group corresponds to the source number listed in the text and graphics in this book. All of these studies were nationwide telephone surveys. Studies 1A through 24 were conducted among a random-digit dial sample of adults, eighteen and older, from within the forty-eight continental states. Studies 25 through 28 were conducted among random samples of the senior pastors of Protestant churches, drawn in a representative fashion from all Protestant denominations. The source number corresponds to the citation following the data presented in this book.

Full-size numbers refer to Data Sources; superscript numbers reference Footnotes.

Study	Date Conducted	Sample Size	Notes:
1A	January 1996	1004	
1	July 1995	1007	
2	January 1995	1006	
3	January and July 1995	2013	combined data of 1 and 2
4	July 1994	1029	
5	January 1994	1205	
6	January and July 1994	2234	combined data of 4 and 5
7	July 1993	1205	
8	January 1993	1205	
9	January and July 1993	2410	combined data of 7 and 8

10	July 1992	1004	
11	January 1992	1013	
12	January and July 1992	2017	combined data of 10 and 11
13	July 1991	1060	
14	January 1991	1005	
15	January and July 1991	2065	combined data of 13 and 14
16	May 1989	602	
17	October 1988	659	
18	December 1986	1200	
19	December 1987	553	
20	May 1982	595	
21	August 1993	601	unchurched adults only
22	August 1993	602	evangelizers only
23	August 1994	3414	
24	November 1994	1164	donors to non-profit organization
25	June 1992	1033	Protestant pastors
26	March 1995	502	Protestant pastors
27	April 1987	487	Protestant pastors
28	April 1994	413	Protestant pastors

1

INDICATORS OF RELIGIOUS SENSITIVITY

RELIGIOUS FAITH, IN GENERAL

Nearly nine out of every ten adults (87 percent) state that their religious faith is very important in their lives. 2

A majority of adults describe themselves as "religious" (60 percent). Notice that one-third of those who say religion plays a vital role in their lives reject the label of "religious." 1

Although most adults consider religion to be a core element in their own lives, the prevailing perception is that most people have experienced a declining degree of spiritual commitment over the past decade. While one-fifth of adults (21 percent) say that the spiritual commitment of Americans has improved in the last ten years, 36 percent say it has remained unchanged and 37 percent say it has gotten worse. 7

Commentary

Cross-cultural studies in developed nations show that Americans are perhaps the most religious people. The key shift that is in process is the movement away from being the most Christian-oriented nation on earth to a nation of people who are religiously diverse and who maintain a high fascination with the spiritual realm.

"Important as the local church is to many Americans, it is not identical with what is understood by religion, which has a meaning that transcends the individual and the local congregation."
—Robert Bellah[1]

"Religion, in short, matters to people; it is real, and so is its influence on human personality."
—Stephen Carter[2]

"The vast majority of Americans consider themselves to be religious and are not afraid to admit it. For most, religion means a personal affirmation of faith in God and an identification with a religious denomination, but it does not necessarily mean joining or being an active member of that particular group. It is more of a private commitment than a shared experience."
—Barry Kosmin and Seymour Lachman[3]

"One of the most remarkable aspects of America's faith is its durability. Despite all of the dramatic social changes of the past half-century—depression, war, the civil rights movement, social unrest, technological change—the religious beliefs and practices of Americans today look very much like the beliefs and practices of the 1930s and 1940s."
—George Gallup, Jr.[4]

"An outstanding feature of America today is that the vast majority of people identify with a religion. This feeling is almost universal, yet it exists within a secular framework, an outer shell of secular values. For what we have witnessed in the latter part of the twentieth century is

the growing secularization of a self-described religious people."
—Barry Kosmin and Seymour Lachman [5]

COMMITMENT TO CHRISTIANITY

Two out of every three adults (67 percent) say they have made a "personal commitment to Jesus Christ that is still important in their life today." [2] This level of commitment has shown a slight increase in the past decade, rising from the 60 percent level in the early and mid-eighties. [20]

People may view themselves as Christian, but their intensity of commitment to the faith is lukewarm. Less than half of its self-proclaimed adherents (41 percent) say they are "absolutely committed" to Christianity. A similar proportion (44 percent) say they are "moderately committed" to the faith. [1]

The hustle and bustle of daily life prevents many people who see themselves as religious, and who acknowledge the significance of religion in their lives, from consciously thinking of themselves as a representative of Jesus Christ. One-quarter of adults (27 percent) say they "always" are mindful of being Christ's representatives; one-sixth (17 percent) say they are "often" aware of that mantel; and one-fourth are "sometimes" conscious of that privilege. The remaining 30 percent of the nation claim they rarely or never think of themselves in this light. [8]

People are less inclined to think of themselves as a representative of their church, synagogue, or religious center than they are to regard themselves as ambassadors of Christ. Overall, just one out of six adults (16 percent) claim they "always" think of themselves as a representative of their church or religious center; one out of seven (14 percent) perceive themselves this way "often"; and one-fourth (24 percent) occasionally have such a perspective. Nearly half of all adults (43 percent) say they rarely or never think of themselves as a representative of their religious group. 8

Americans are quite label-conscious and are careful about the descriptions they adopt for themselves. When asked which, if any, of several different terms they would use to describe themselves, 18 percent chose the term "evangelical." Almost twice as many people (29 percent) chose the term "fundamentalist." 1 A more popular religious term of these three was "born again," selected by almost four out of ten adults (39 percent). 4 The proportion of people who call themselves born-again Christians has remained unchanged over the past decade. (See chapter 7 for a further discussion of matters related to immortality.)

Commentary

Much of American Christianity is nominal in nature. Americans like to have a term to summarize their religiosity, and "Christian" remains the label of choice, even if their commitment to biblical Christianity is waning. With loyalty rapidly becoming a cultural artifact, commitment to a local church is also on the decline.

"Much of the old spiritual style prior to the 1960s depended on homogeneity, upon assent to the details of a grand theological or philosophical system. But this has all changed in the intervening years. Greater attention to spiritual quest, an expanded number of religious options, and a consumer culture have all contributed to 'multilayered' styles of belief and practice."

—Wade Clark Roof [6]

4

RELATING TO A DEITY

Most Americans would like to have a serious involvement with their deity. Three-quarters of all adults (74 percent) say it would be "very desirable" to have a "close relationship with God." 7

Two-thirds of all adults (68 percent) claim they have felt that they were in the presence of God at some time in their lives. In fact, many of those people regularly sense the presence of God: half believe they are in His presence at least one time each week. 5

Commentary

Americans enjoy being known to and favored by those in power. While many people are confused about the nature and purposes of God, and growing numbers are not quite convinced of the omnipotence of God, most adults remain desirous of having positive interactions with their deity.

THE SIGNIFICANCE OF SPIRITUALITY

Americans are evenly split on the issue of whether or not a person can lead a full and satisfying life even if he or she does not pursue personal spiritual development. This constitutes a decline from the past, as national surveys conducted in the fifties and sixties suggest that a substantial majority of the population of that era believed that pursuit of spiritual maturity was a prerequisite to life fulfillment. 4

Two out of three adults say they are "absolutely certain" that in times of personal crisis they can count on God to take care of them. 5

Not quite half of the public (45 percent) strongly agree that the Christian faith is relevant to their lives these days. An additional one-third state that they agree with this notion, but only moderately so. 7

Commentary

Increasingly, faith commitment is viewed as a hobby rather than as a necessity for personal wholeness. Given their relative ignorance about supernatural matters, and their skepticism of institutions (such as churches), true spiritual commitment is deemed to be a bonus, not a necessity. Adults' mental portrait of success in life resembles an aerial view of Washington, D.C.: the city is circled by the Beltway, with a substantial number of feeder highways leading to the encircling road, which permits entry to the city. Any of the feeder roads will get you to your destination; the options are equivalent, the choice is personal and idiosyncratic.

"America is spiritually thirsty. After decades of advancing secularism, oppressive communism, and declining spiritual interest, a spiritual awakening is sweeping the world. America is part of this awakening. There is a fascinating mix of disillusionment, post-secularism, generational depression, fear about the future, and return to fundamentalism."
—Leith Anderson 7

"Why do people return to organized religion? Unquestionably, the most frequently cited reasons have to do with family life. . . . A second

set of reasons has to do with a personal quest for meaning—for something to believe in, for answers to questions about life. Feelings of emptiness and loneliness, whether or not they are articulated in this way, lead people in such pursuits. A third cluster of responses emphasizes the importance of belonging to a community."
—Wade Clark Roof[8]

"Religious individualism is, in many ways, appropriate in our kind of society. It is no more going to go away than is secular individualism. Ours is a society that requires people to be strong and independent."
—Robert Bellah[9]

"Religion counts in American society. It is linked to the voluntarism and individualism that was recognized by Alexis de Tocqueville over a hundred and fifty years ago. This has led to American Exceptionalism. Religion in American society plays a number of different roles, from organizing social authority to providing a sense of community and group solidarity."
—Barry Kosmin and Seymour Lachman[10]

SPREADING THE WORD

Although more than four out of five adults believe that every person has the right to choose and to practice a religious faith in a manner that suits them, only half as many (42 percent) enjoy the ability of others to experience their religious freedom by proselytizing. Overall, nearly half of the population (42 percent) say that when another person tries to explain their religious beliefs, it is "usually annoying."[10]

Percentage of Americans Who Have Described Themselves as "Religious"

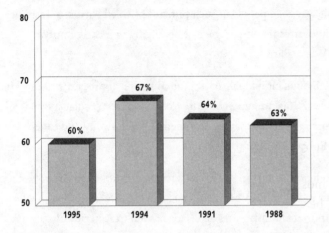

Percentage of Americans Who Claim They Have Made a "Personal Commitment" to Jesus Christ that Is Still Important Today

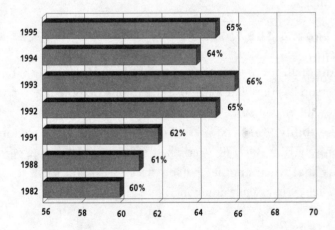

2

FAITH GROUP OF CHOICE

Almost nine out of ten people (85 percent) consider themselves
to be Christian. Shifts in denominational allegiances, however,
have reshaped perceptions of group loyalties. In the sixties and
seventies, more than 60 percent described themselves
as Protestant. Today, only 35 percent use that label for
themselves. The reason: increasing numbers of people who
attend Protestant churches describe themselves as "Christian"
rather than "Protestant."

Protestantism remains the most prolific faith group in the
nation. Roughly 160 million Americans are associated with
Protestant churches.

The proportion of people who define themselves as Catholic has
remained constant during the past decade—in the 25–30 percent
range. In total, America has about seventy-five million Catholics,
including children.

The Jewish population has remained at about 2 percent of the
nation. The Mormon population has increased over the past

decade to the same level. Each of these faith groups now encompasses approximately four million adult followers.

Eastern religions remain small on the religious landscape of America. Less than 1 percent of the population are associated with each of the largest of the Eastern faith groups. The Muslim faith has become the largest of the Eastern faith groups to penetrate America, claiming roughly two million followers.

There are four times as many atheists as there are Jews or Mormons. Overall, 8 percent of American adults currently claim to be atheist. There has been a small increase in atheism in the past decade, rising from about 5 percent in 1984.

Despite media reports to the contrary, 66 percent of American adults believe that the United States is a "Christian nation." 14

Commentary

While the growth in the number of Americans associated with a Protestant church has stalled, the U.S. still has more Protestant adherents than any other nation. Growth patterns in several African and Asian nations indicate that this status may not last for long. The U.S. is also among the ten largest Catholic contingents in the world.

"An observer of the religious scene today is struck by the proliferation of groups organized around specific life situations, crises, and needs." —Wade Clark Roof [1]

"America is still a denominational society. The best 'fit' for the data is a model which indicates stability of affiliation with the identity Protestant, Catholic, or Jew. In short, denominationalism has not

changed much, although patterns of denominational affiliation have altered dramatically."
—Andrew Greeley[2]

FEELINGS ABOUT FAITH GROUPS

Most people (85 percent) believe that Christians have a generally positive influence on American society. Six out of ten adults (58 percent) believe that Jews have a positive influence on the nation. A minority of adults contend that each of the next five largest faith groups have a positive influence on our society. Forty-three percent approve of the influence of Mormons; 29 percent have a positive image of the impact of Buddhists; 28 percent regarding Muslims; 21 percent related to Scientologists; and 14 percent regarding atheists. [1]

Six out of ten Americans believe that atheists have a generally negative influence on America. [1]

Most adults have moderately favorable attitudes toward the major denominational groups in the U.S. A majority hold favorable impressions of Baptist churches (65 percent either very favorable or somewhat favorable impressions), Methodist churches (60 percent) and the Roman Catholic church (59 percent). Half maintain a favorable view of Presbyterian churches (50 percent). A minority have a favorable image of Lutheran churches (47 percent) and the Mormon church (27 percent). While the Salvation Army is a church, and draws the most positive reviews of all (92 percent favorable), relatively few adults realize it is a church; most people perceive the Salvation Army to be a social service organization. [13]

Even the most widely appreciated churches—Baptist churches—have a very favorable impression in the minds of just three out of every ten adults (29 percent). 13

People's Opinions of Major Church Groups

	favorable		unfavorable		no
	very	somewhat	somewhat	very	opinion
Presbyterian	12%	38%	9%	4%	38%
Baptist	29	36	10	5	20
Lutheran	12	35	8	5	41
Methodist	18	42	8	4	29
Roman Catholic	23	36	16	7	18
Salvation Army	57	35	2	1	5
Mormon Church	6	21	18	19	36

Commentary

Regardless of their flagging commitment to Christianity, overall most adults possess a generally positive view of the Christian faith. They are relatively less informed about the different Protestant church groups; large proportions of them said they did not have an opinion of various denominational groups because they know little or nothing about them. Despite recent calls for openness to cultural diversity or pluralism, most Americans remain suspicious—if not negative—toward faiths other than Christianity and its progenitor, Judaism.

PROTESTANT-CATHOLIC RELATIONS

Four out of five Americans (79 percent) believe that Protestants and Catholics should put aside their religious differences and work together. Ten percent believe the two groups should maintain a cordial relationship but recognize their religious differences and not work together. Just 4 percent suggest that the two groups acknowledge that they have little in common and overtly compete with each other. 1

Catholics are more likely to be willing to work together. Ninety percent said it's time for Protestants and Catholics to work harmoniously, compared to similar sentiments expressed by only 78 percent of Protestants. Just 61 percent of evangelicals were supportive of such cooperation. 1

Commentary

To the average American, the divide between Catholics and Protestants is a historical issue, not a modern-day necessity. Few comprehend the basic disagreement which caused Luther and other sixteenth-century religious leaders to initiate the Reformation. Americans are more likely to perceive the primary differences between the Protestant and Catholic churches to be stylistic and organizational rather than theological.

"To bring God's truth about the public good into the public square and to resist the abortionists and mercy-killers, the relativists and tyrants, Christians must stand together. The controversies that have divided [Protestant and Catholic] believers for nearly five hundred years are real, to be sure, and none of them is to be minimized. However, the divisions between us are not the battle of the hour, when hosts of secularists and relativists threaten to sweep away the last trace of Christian truth, thought, and influence from our culture. Indeed,

the controversies that divide us are far less significant than the common threat that confronts us."
—Charles Colson[3]

"For almost five centuries now Catholics and Protestants have lived with crippling dichotomies, such as that between the Bible and tradition, and between ritual and spiritual experience. The most grievously crippling dichotomy, however, is that between the gospel and the Church."
—Richard John Neuhaus[4]

A SUPERIOR FAITH

Two-thirds of all adults (68 percent) believe that the Christian faith has "all the answers to leading a successful life." 11 Six out of ten people (58 percent) also contend that there is no single religious faith which has "all the answers to life's questions and challenges." 4

A slight majority (54 percent) reject the notion that "all religious faiths teach equally valid truths." A growing proportion of adults (currently 40 percent) believe this view is accurate. 4

Commentary

Because increasing numbers of people turn to religion to provide them with insights and abilities to meet tangible goals, faith is used by many people as a means to a worldly, rather than eternal, end. There is also the reality that as Americans become more sensitive to style and structure, rather than substance, the belief systems of major faith groups become somewhat obscured, and millions of adults have embraced the philosophy that the key is to be religious, regardless of the choice of religion.

RELIGIOUS TOLERANCE

People are only moderately convinced that Christian churches are tolerant of people who have different ideas than those taught in the church. Just one-fifth (19 percent) strongly agree that such tolerance exists. Forty percent agree somewhat, 20 percent disagree somewhat, while 12 percent strongly disagree that Christian churches are tolerant of people with different ideas. 14

People who do not attend church or religious services are more likely to think that Christian churches are intolerant than tolerant. Their spin: Christian churches not only discard ideas they don't like, but they discard the people who possess those ideas. 21

Commentary

Tolerance has become a major bone of contention in the religious arena. Christian churches that promote absolutes and which refuse to change their rules, traditions, and theological interpretations to accommodate the times are sometimes characterized by outsiders as "rigid" or intolerant. With cultural literacy on the decline and globalism on the incline, the result is the homogenization of the world's unique cultures. Religious groups receive the same type of pressure to move to the middle, rather than to remain distinct.

"Diversity of practice has been seen as legitimate because religion is perceived as a matter of individual choice. . . ."
—Robert Bellah[5]

Faith Groups with Which People Associate
(by percentages)

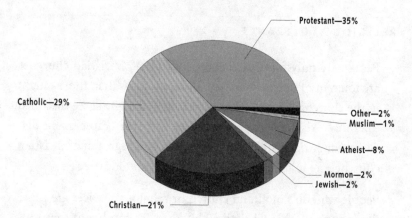

Protestant—35%

Catholic—29%

Other—2%
Muslim—1%

Atheist—8%

Mormon—2%
Jewish—2%

Christian—21%

Perspectives on the General Influence of
Faith Groups on American Society

	Positive	Negative	Both	Not sure
Christians	85%	4%	4%	6%
Jews	58	15	4	23
Muslims	28	33	4	35
Mormons	43	27	5	26
Scientologists	21	39	3	38
Buddhists	29	33	2	35
Atheists	14	61	4	22

3

INDICATORS ABOUT RELIGIOUS BELIEF

PERCEPTIONS OF THE BIBLE

Six out of ten adults (58 percent) maintain that the Bible is "totally accurate in all of its teachings." 1A

Almost half of the population (45 percent) believe that the Bible is "absolutely accurate and everything in it can be taken literally." 4

While millions believe the Bible is accurate in its recording of information, a substantial number of adults do not believe that all of the information is relevant for today. One out of every five adults (18 percent) contend that one of the renowned portions of the Bible—the Ten Commandments—is "not relevant for people living today." 11

There is much misunderstanding about the history of the Bible. For instance, four out of every ten adults (38 percent) believe that the entire Bible was written several decades after Jesus' death and resurrection. While this appears to be true for the New Testament, the entire Old Testament was written hundreds of years prior to the birth of Jesus Christ. 4

Commentary

The Bible maintains a revered position in our society. However, its status as an unquestioned book of religious truths is slowly eroding. As time goes on, fewer Americans know where the Bible came from, what it contains, or how much credence to give its words.

"The decline in Bible reading is due to many factors: the feeling that the Bible is inaccessible; the belief that it has little to say to today's world; a decline in reading in general; and less emphasis on religious training."
—George Gallup, Jr.[1]

GOD

More than nine out of ten adults (93 percent) say they believe that God exists. [1] While perceptions of God and people's connection to God have changed over time, this level of trust in the existence of a deity has remained unchanged for decades.

When it comes to defining what "God" means to people, a surprisingly large proportion—nearly three out of ten—describe a deity other than the God portrayed in the Bible. The other depictions of God include: a state of higher consciousness that an individual may reach (11 percent endorse this description of "god"); the total realization of personal human potential (8 percent); the belief that there are many gods, each with its own power and authority (3 percent); everyone is their own god (3 percent); and 2 percent who maintain that there is no such thing as God. [1]

Commentary

God means many things to many people. While most Americans buy into the notion of a higher power or supreme being of some sort, the consensus as to the identity and nature of that authority is crumbling. Currently, though, there remains a consensus about God: i.e., He is the deity described in the Bible.

"It is not surprising that many in this generation are asking fundamental questions about the meaning and existence of God. To explore the inner self and its relations to the larger world is to open up possibilities of new symbolic constructions, or 'pictures', by which humans imagine the ultimate force shaping life."
—Wade Clark Roof[2]

JESUS CHRIST

It is the rare American who thinks of Jesus Christ as a religious figment of the imagination. Nine out of ten adults (88 percent) believe that He was a real person. [4]

The role of Mary, the mother of Jesus, is secure in the minds of most Americans. In fact, almost nine out of ten people—85 percent—believe that Jesus Christ was born to a virgin. Even 75 percent of the people who do not embrace Jesus as their savior believe that He was born to a virgin. [4]

The vast majority (85 percent) believe that Jesus Christ was crucified, died, and rose from the dead and is spiritually alive today. [8]

Most people (82 percent) believe that when Jesus was on earth He was as much a human being as they are. 10

Large proportions of adults—although still a minority—are not convinced of the perfect nature of Christ. More than one-third (37 percent) say that Jesus made mistakes when He was on earth.5 More significantly, though, 44 percent claim that when He lived on earth, "Jesus Christ was human and committed sins, like other people." 1

Many born-again Christians struggle with the idea of Jesus being sinless. One out of four adults (26 percent) who are born again—i.e., people who contend that Jesus Christ is the spiritual savior of humankind, and who have personally embraced Him as their savior—claim that He committed sins during His tenure on earth. 1

Relatively few people are aware of Jesus' lineage. Just one-third of all adults (36 percent) are aware that Jesus Christ was related to King David. 4

The idea of a second coming of Jesus Christ is real to most Americans. Seven out of ten (70 percent) believe that someday Jesus will come back. 10

Commentary

Most people have traditional Christian views about Jesus Christ: His historicity, virgin birth, humanity and deity, resurrection from the dead, etc. Many adults, however, remain uncertain about the perfect (i.e., sinless) nature of Christ, and have little knowledge regarding the prophecies preceding His life and death. Nevertheless, most Americans believe in Christ, to some degree, as the savior of humankind who will return for those who have gained His favor.

HOLY SPIRIT

While the Holy Spirit remains a relatively mysterious figure to many people, four out of five adults (82 percent) believe that "God's Holy Spirit lives within people who have accepted Jesus Christ as their savior." [4]

EVANGELISM

Three out of ten adults (30 percent) strongly agree that they have a personal responsibility to tell other people their religious beliefs. Overall, about half of all adults (48 percent) strongly or moderately believe that they have such a responsibility. [1]

Individuals who have never attended college are 65 percent more likely than those who have attended or graduated from college to strongly agree that they have a responsibility to share the nature of their faith with others. [1]

Commentary

Proselytizing is controversial, even in a nation birthed in the name and defense of religious liberty. Christians often feel they have a duty to share their beliefs with non-Christians. Such a commitment to leading others to their faith is not as widely shared among adherents of the Eastern religions that have come to America. As the nation becomes more concerned about issues pertaining to privacy, though, evangelistic efforts may become even more controversial.

SIN, SATAN, AND EVIL

Most Americans do not believe in Satan (or, the devil). Six out of ten adults (58 percent) believe that Satan "is not a living being but is a symbol of evil." 1

One-third of adults (32 percent) contend that there are some crimes, sins, or other things people might do which cannot be forgiven by God. 8

About one-fifth of the adult population (19 percent) believe that "the whole idea of sin is outdated." 11

Commentary

While people accept the existence of "sin," they do not take it as seriously as they once did, nor do they accept rigid definitions of sinful behavior. This is tied to the growing perception that the Christian depiction of Satan as a living force of evil is not to be taken literally. As Americans become more self-focused and self-reliant, even in spiritual matters, they are willing to take credit for both the good and the bad in their lives—success as well as sin. This means that Satan—and God—are often excluded from the equation.

"Most of us spend the first six days of each week sowing wild oats;

then we go to church on Sunday and pray for crop failure."
—Fred Allen [3]

PRAYER

Americans believe in the power and impact of prayer. Four out of
five (82 percent) believe that "prayer can change what happens in
a person's life." [4]

Nine out of ten adults (89 percent) agree that "there is a god who
watches over you and answers your prayers." [14]

A majority of adults believe that "all people pray to the same god
or spirit, no matter what name they use for that spiritual being."
Most recently, 53 percent agreed with that statement, a drop from
64 percent three years earlier. [4, 14]

Commentary

For most people, prayer is a form of spiritual gambling: you make
your needs and desires known and hope for the best. Our
understanding of prayer is generally divorced from a deeper
knowledge of the theological role of prayer.

"The one difference I see between churchgoers and those with deep
spiritual faith is the latter meet frequently in small groups in
fellowship, prayer and mutual support. In this setting, people can see
the power of prayer, and make the exciting discovery that God really
cares about them personally."
—Michael McManus [4]

"It's amazing how many coincidences occur when one begins to pray."
—Anonymous

SPIRITUAL GIFTS

Most people (71 percent) say they have heard of spiritual gifts, which are the supernatural abilities given by God, through His Holy Spirit, to those who believe in Jesus Christ. However, comparatively few adults who have heard of these gifts believe that they, personally, have a spiritual gift or are able to identify their gift. 2

Among those who have heard of spiritual gifts, 31 percent can name a spiritual gift they believe they possess. That's the equivalent of 22 percent of the total adult public identifying a spiritual gift they possess. 2

The most commonly claimed gifts are teaching (7 percent believe they have this gift); helps/service (7 percent); faith (4 percent); knowledge (4 percent); mercy (4 percent); and tongues (3 percent). 2

When those who have heard of spiritual gifts are asked to identify their spiritual gift, 31 percent of the population list characteristics or qualities which are not spiritual gifts identified in the Bible. Another 12 percent claim they do not have a spiritual gift. Among the characteristics listed as gifts, but which are not identified in the Bible, were being a good person, having a sense of humor, being in good health, friendliness, honesty, the ability to listen to others, being patient, and having a nice personality. 2

Commentary

One obvious reason why many churches and church people labor in vain, despite their good intentions, is their ignorance of spiritual gifts. While Christian theology indicates that believers are specially empowered for specific types of service, our research has consistently shown that millions of church volunteers operate in areas other than those of their gift and thus struggle to succeed. Notice, too, that less than 3 percent of all believers acknowledge having the gift of leadership.

"Previous to 1970, seminary graduates characteristically left their institutions knowing little or nothing about spiritual gifts. Now, such a state of affairs would generally be regarded as a deficiency in ministerial training."
—C. Peter Wagner[5]

SPEAKING IN TONGUES

One of the most controversial spiritual gifts—tongues—is also one of the best known. Almost three-fourths of the nation's adults (72 percent) have heard of the gift of tongues. Four out of ten adults (39 percent) have heard someone else speak in tongues. Seven percent say that they have personally spoken in tongues. [2]

Tongues is more prevalent in Christian circles than many people realize. Among born again Christians, 16 percent say they have spoken in tongues. Among evangelicals, 27 percent have spoken in tongues. Among Catholics, 3 percent have spoken in tongues, significantly less than the 16 percent among those who attend

Protestant churches. Tongues are not common among Baptists (5 percent) or those who attend mainline Protestant churches (6 percent). Among adults who watch religious TV programs, 18 percent have spoken in tongues. 2

Perspectives on the gift of tongues vary. One-fourth of all adults (27 percent) believe that God gives the gift of tongues to some people, but not to others. A similar proportion (23 percent) believe that every Christian can have this gift, if they ask God for it. One out of five adults (19 percent) deny the existence of the gift, saying that "there is not now, and never has been, a gift of tongues." One out of seven people (14 percent) say that this gift was given to some people immediately after the death of Jesus Christ, but that the gift is no longer operative. The remaining one-fifth (18 percent) do not know what to believe about the gift of tongues. 2

Among those who have heard of the gift of tongues, viewpoints vary widely. For instance:

- 73 percent say that speaking in tongues is biblical, but it is not necessary for a Christian to lead a full Christian life;

- 40 percent say that if they were to speak in tongues, they would be frightened by the experience;

- 38 percent say that speaking in tongues is a sign that a person has truly let God take total control of his/her life;

- 35 percent say people who speak in tongues are usually sincere, but are more likely involved in an emotional outburst that is neither biblical nor of God;

- 28 percent say even if a person believes they are speaking in tongues, it is not an experience directed by God;

- 23 percent say that if they did speak in tongues, they would be too embarrassed to let other people know;

- 23 percent say speaking in tongues is a sign of spiritual maturity;

- 8 percent say speaking in tongues is evidence of demonic possession. 2

Commentary

There remains a significant divide within the Christian community regarding the existence and role of tongues. Much of the division is based on an emotional reaction to the use of tongues, rather than a theological response to this gift.

MIRACLES

Most people take the Bible at face value when it comes to the descriptions of the miracles that took place. Three out of four adults (73 percent) believe that "all of the miracles described in the Bible actually took place." 4

ASTROLOGY AND NEW AGE SPIRITUALITY

Relatively few people put much stock in astrology. Just 8 percent believe astrology can accurately predict the future. 4

While "new age" adherents contend that crystals are a source of supernatural power, only 7 percent of the adult public supports that view. 4

Tarot cards are deemed to be a reliable source of guidance for life decisions by 9 percent of the public. 4

One of the most intriguing revelations regarding the spread of new age thinking relates to perspectives of deity. While two-thirds of all adults maintain a relatively traditional concept of God, one out of four adults have moved closer to a "new age" interpretation of a supreme being. This group is comprised of the 11 percent who define God as "a state of higher consciousness that a person may reach;" the 8 percent who also define god in personal terms, saying it is "the total realization of personal, human potential;" the 3 percent who say there are many gods, territorial in nature, each with its own power and authority; and the 3 percent who believe that each person is god. 1

Commentary

The so-called "New Age" faith community is difficult to evaluate since it has no identifiable leader, geographic center, holy books, or dominant churches. However, there is a small but stable core—roughly one out of every five adults—who are most closely aligned with the belief patterns and lifestyle systems advocated by new age teaching.

"The rediscovery of inner experience puts young Americans, often armed with Carl Jung and Abraham Maslow, more in touch with themselves: asking questions about the meaning of life; peak experiences; searching to find ways of feeling, and not just thinking about, their relationship to the surrounding universe; and exploring the authority and healing power of the nonrational, the mythic, and the dreamlike. The result is that psychology has become the vehicle for an emerging form of religiousness. . . ."
—Wade Clark Roof [6]

"In turbulent times, in times of great change, people head for the two extremes: fundamentalism and personal, spiritual experience. . . . With no membership lists or even a coherent philosophy or dogma, it is difficult to define or measure the unorganized New Age movement. But in every major U.S. and European city thousands who seek insight and personal growth cluster around a metaphysical bookstore, a spiritual teacher, or an educational center."
—John Naisbitt [7]

"While America may be among the most religiously diverse nations, one can observe a process of Americanization at work on all of its religions."
—Barry Kosmin and Seymour Lachman [8]

The Changing Way in Which Americans Define God

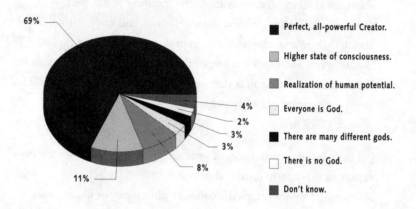

- ■ Perfect, all-powerful Creator.
- □ Higher state of consciousness.
- ▨ Realization of human potential.
- ▫ Everyone is God.
- ■ There are many different gods.
- □ There is no God.
- ■ Don't know.

69%
4%
2%
3%
3%
8%
11%

Most People are in the Dark Regarding Spiritual Gifts

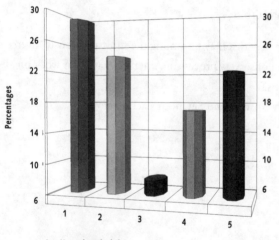

Percentages

1. Never heard of them.
2. Don't know what their gift is.
3. Claim they don't have one.
4. Identified one or more spiritual gifts.
5. Named only gifts not listed in the Bible.

Speaking in Tongues Is Controversial

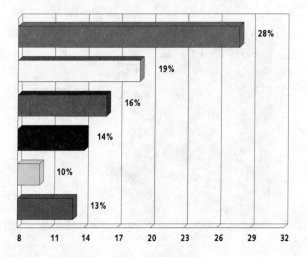

28%

19%

16%

14%

10%

13%

8   11   14   17   20   23   26   29   32

■ Have never heard of speaking in tongues.

□ God gives the gift of tongues to some, but not to others.

■ Every Christian can have this gift.

■ There is not now, and never has been, a gift of tongues.

▨ Gift was given to some after the Resurrection; gift is no longer operative.

▨ Do not know what to believe about tongues.

What Do People Believe in?

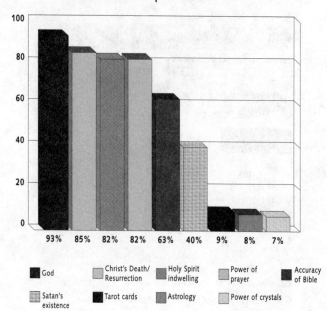

93% 85% 82% 82% 63% 40% 9% 8% 7%

■ God	Christ's Death/ Resurrection	Holy Spirit indwelling	Power of prayer	■ Accuracy of Bible
Satan's existence	■ Tarot cards	Astrology	Power of crystals	

4

CHURCH ATTENDANCE

From the mid-eighties to the mid-nineties, church attendance was on a rollercoaster ride. In 1986, 42 percent of adults attended a church service during a typical week in January. Attendance rose steadily, reaching a peak of 49 percent in 1991, before beginning a very slow but steady descent back to 42 percent in January 1995.

The traditional pattern of Catholics being more likely than Protestants to attend church during the weekend has disappeared. Since 1993, church-going habits have been the same for both groups. This is largely attributable to a relaxation of attendance among Catholics, more than a surge in attendance among Protestants.

The frequency with which people attend church services has not changed since the turn of the decade. On average, about one-third attend every week; one-third attend one to three weekends each month; and the remaining one-third never attend, except for special occasions such as weddings and funerals.

About sixty to sixty-five million adults, and an additional twenty to twenty-five million people age seventeen or younger, fail to attend church services, other than those for special events such as weddings or funerals, during a typical six-month period. Although many of those individuals are church "members," they do not get involved in church activity. The proportion of the unchurched has been slowly rising since the late eighties.

Commentary

Church attendance rose from the mid-eighties to mid-1991 due to the desire of Baby Boomers to incorporate spirituality into their lives. Many were driven by the urge to expose their children to religion; others were searching for meaning and purpose in life, which they had not found through focus on career, materialism, and other exploits.

By the middle of 1991, however, Boomers, in particular, began to sense that the traditional religious groups (e.g. Catholicism and Protestantism) did not have the answers after which they were seeking. A series of cataclysmic events—the demise of the Soviet Union, America's economic problems, the ideological battles of candidates Bush, Clinton, and Perot, the recognition (through Magic Johnson's public acknowledgment of having been infected with HIV) that AIDS can strike heterosexuals, the loss of lives and billions of dollars of damage caused by Hurricane Andrew and the flooding of the Mississippi—happened in such a contracted time period, and hit with such force, that millions of Boomers began to question the nature of their God and to doubt the value of their faith. Consequently, their church attendance became more erratic.

Meanwhile, Baby Busters have shown an inclination to reject the church right from the start. The result: slowly declining church attendance among the adult population.

CHURCH PREFERENCE

Since 1982, the denomination of the church that people attend most often has shown little change for several major denominations, and significant change for others. The churches that have remained stable are the Roman Catholic (23 percent of all adults claim this as their church); Baptist (29 percent); and Church of God (2 percent). The bodies experiencing the greatest decline have been the Methodist (from 12 percent in 1982 to 8 percent in 1995); Lutheran (from 7 percent down to 4 percent); Presbyterian (from 5 percent down to 3 percent) churches.

Adults are much more likely to change churches than to switch denominations. Three out of four adults (76 percent) say they currently attend a church that is affiliated with the same denomination of the church they attended when they were young. Less than one-third of all adults are attending the same church in which they were raised. 9

Most people attend the same church every time they go to church services, but that sense of loyalty is declining. Currently, just six out of ten church-goers (61 percent) always attend the same church. Three out of ten (30 percent) usually attend the same church, but occasionally try other churches. The other one out of ten (9 percent) intentionally divide their attendance among two or more churches. This latter group is growing slowly but steadily. 11

Commentary

As a consumer mentality invades the religious domain, "brand loyalty" among churches is disappearing. More often than not, people are asking what the church has to offer them, without much regard for what they can invest in the church as a community of believers called to be one body.

"Mainline churches fare well in stable eras but decline in times of great change."
—John Naisbitt [1]

CHURCH PROGRAM INVOLVEMENT

Adult Sunday school attendance is on the decline. One out of four adults (23 percent) attended such classes in 1991. The proportion has dipped to one out of six (17 percent) in 1996. 1A, 14

Christian education classes held on the same day as church worship services is a Protestant phenomenon. Three out of ten adults (28 percent) associated with a Protestant church attend such classes on any given week. Less than one out of ten Catholics do so. 1A

Contrary to popular opinion, there is virtually no drop off in Sunday school attendance witnessed during the summer months. For instance, during the winter of 1995, adult attendance was 17 percent; during the summer months, it was 16 percent.

During a typical week, one out of every six adults (17 percent) is involved in some type of small group that meets regularly for Bible study, prayer, or Christian fellowship, other than a Sunday school class or twelve-step group. This involvement is much more common among Protestants (24 percent) than Catholics (7 percent). 1A

Commentary

Christian education is being restructured. Instead of attending formal classes on the church campus, millions of people are attending small groups in people's homes for a more relaxed educational experience. While our research shows that small groups are struggling to become a permanent fixture, due to difficulties with the quality of teaching, lack of in-group leadership, disconnectedness from the church body, and efforts to accomplish too much during the group time, many church leaders hold out hope that as churches address cultural changes and the need to "re-engineer" the ministry, small group ministries will arise as a glue that holds the local body together relationally.

"The small group movement is a major social trend that reflects the micro-segmentation of American society. Americans are seeking meaningful relationships out of deep-felt loneliness. Decades of mobility, divorce, blended families, and individual isolation have multiplied the list of legitimate felt needs, driving people together into groups to help one another meet these needs."
—Leith Anderson [2]

"Religion is one of the most important of the many ways in which Americans 'get involved' in the life of their community and society." —Robert Bellah[3]

TIME COMMITMENT

For most adults (53 percent) the amount of time they typically devote to church-related activity remains constant. However, almost half of all adults are revising the time they commit to church. More than one-quarter (28 percent) are spending less time in church-related endeavors; 16 percent are allocating more time for such pursuits. [5]

CHURCH PRIORITIES

Pastors of Protestant churches indicate that the top priorities of the church for the coming year were: worship (mentioned as one of the three major priorities by 52 percent); evangelism (43 percent); Christian education (41 percent); youth ministry (28 percent); missions (18 percent); children's ministry (16 percent); community social action (12 percent); discipleship (11 percent); congregational care (11 percent); and small group ministries (11 percent). [26]

Church Attendance in a Typical Week Is Declining

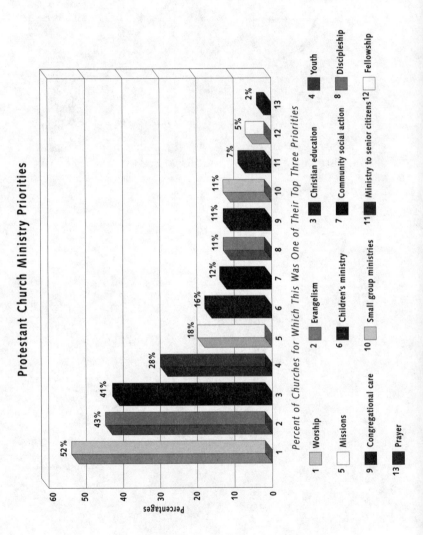

Protestant Church Ministry Priorities

Percent of Churches for Which This Was One of Their Top Three Priorities

1 Worship	2 Evangelism	3 Christian education	4 Youth
5 Missions	6 Children's ministry	7 Community social action	8 Discipleship
9 Congregational care	10 Small group ministries	11 Ministry to senior citizens	12 Fellowship
13 Prayer		

Church Fidelity to the Same Church Is on the Wane

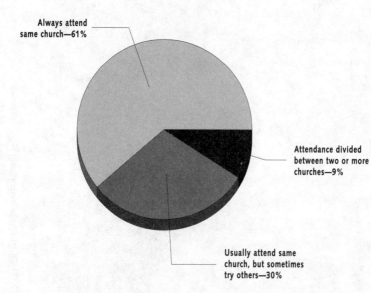

Always attend same church—61%

Attendance divided between two or more churches—9%

Usually attend same church, but sometimes try others—30%

5

INDICATORS OF SATISFACTION WITH CHURCHES

OVERVIEW OF SATISFACTION

Most adults do not have a lot of confidence in Christian churches. Less than half (43 percent) said they have a lot of confidence in Christian churches; 37 percent said they have "some"; 13 percent said they do not have much confidence in them; and 4 percent said they have no confidence in these religious bodies. The remaining 3 percent did not know. 14

When asked to rate their church on various aspects of ministry, there is not a single attribute among those tested for which at least half of all church attenders describe their church as doing an "excellent" job.

The elements of their church experience which people find most satisfying are the friendliness of the people in the congregation (46 percent said this is "excellent"); the care and concern demonstrated by the church staff (45 percent); the preaching (44 percent); the music in the worship service (44 percent); and the buildings and physical facilities of the church (43 percent). 14

The aspects of church ministry which received the lowest ratings were the quality of teaching in church classes and the programs for young people. 14

Ratings of Church Elements
(*Denotes less than one-half of one percent)

	Excellent	Good	Average	Below average	Poor
Friendliness of the congregation	46%	40%	12%	2%	1%
Concern and care by clergy/staff	45	40	11	1	1
Preaching	44	41	12	1	1
Music in worship services	44	39	13	2	1
Buildings, facilities	43	42	12	1	1
Overall management of the church	35	46	15	1	*
Programs for young children	32	40	15	2	2
Quality of teaching in classes	28	47	13	1	2
Programs for teenagers	24	37	17	5	3

Commentary

People's reactions to the quality of their church experience were rather lukewarm. While they feel that most activities are done with excellence or good quality, still their confidence is slipping and their commitment is waning. It is as if the key to their experience is the great missing ingredient: the presence of God, which is infrequently sensed. Without that, much of what takes place is simply human performance of rituals.

"Americans have become more critical of their churches and synagogues over the past decade. A large majority believes the churches are too concerned with internal organizational issues and not sufficiently concerned with spiritual matters."
—George Gallup, Jr.[1]

MEMBERSHIP

Fewer people are members of a church, synagogue, or religious center than used to be the case. While studies conducted in the fifties suggest that nearly 80 percent of Americans were members of a local religious institution then, just 60 percent claim formal membership today. 7

Many people are more likely to cite church membership as important than they are to be members themselves. Three out of four adults (76 percent) agree that membership in a church, synagogue, or religious center is important. 7 That figure is a drop from 84 percent in 1989. 16

Commentary

Membership is not especially relevant in today's society. The demand for open-ended, long-term commitment is unattractive to people. While the notion of church membership is only slowly dying, the reality of such formal commitment to the church is dying a much faster death—especially as household transience, which requires alignment with a new local body, defines 15–20 percent of all households each year.

"While Americans attach great importance to religion, they do not equate religion with church membership or attendance."
—George Gallup, Jr. [2]

PERFORMANCE BY THE CLERGY

Although few people (9 percent) believe that the clergy are doing an excellent job, a large proportion (58 percent) characterize their performance as good. Just 16 percent describe their performance as "not too good" and 7 percent say it is poor. One out of ten adults (11 percent) don't know how to rate the clergy. In context, this places clergy among the highest rated professionals in the nation, below judges and doctors but above teachers, attorneys, professors, and business executives. [7]

People place higher demands on the clergy than they place upon themselves. Three out of four adults (73 percent) admit that they expect clergy to live up to higher standards of moral and ethical conduct than they expect of themselves or of other people. [10]

Commentary

To their credit, the clergy are held to higher standards—and, generally, are perceived to reach those standards. The real issue is how church-going people can expect a higher level of performance from individuals who are called to holiness by the same God which they, themselves, serve.

CHURCH LOYALTY

Half of all adults (49 percent) believe it is very desirable to "be part of a local church"; with three out of ten (29 percent) describing this as somewhat desirable. Two out of ten say it is not desirable. 7

People are moderately committed to remaining part of the denomination to which their current church belongs. Just less than half of all adults (45 percent) say they are very committed to attending a church associated with that denomination and 37 percent are somewhat committed to this practice. Overall, only 15 percent are not committed to such an affiliation. (Four percent are not sure how stable their commitment is.) 7

The vast majority of people have no intention of departing from their current church. Seven out of ten adults said they are not at all likely to change from the church they currently attend most often to another church, and one out of eight said such a change is not too likely. In fact, just 4 percent said they are very likely to change, with 11 percent somewhat likely. 11

Commentary

As denominational ties continue to dissolve, we find that church-hopping is usually a response to change—e.g., personnel changes, stylistic shifts, friends moving, or teaching which is deemed heretical. These changes cause otherwise complacent people to reassign their church loyalty and involvement. There is a constant reshuffling of the deck: at any given moment, there are four to six million church attenders seeking a new church home.

"The day is fast disappearing when people choose churches because of the name of the denomination, the mode of baptism, or the system of theology. But that doesn't mean that diversity will disappear. The new diversity is based on style of worship, socioeconomic status, racial/ethnic/language background, the variety of services that a local church offers, and the list keeps getting longer."
—Leith Anderson[3]

"Americans take a very independent approach to religion. Their faith must make sense to them, and it must reflect the values of freedom they assume in their daily social and political lives."
—George Gallup, Jr.[4]

"The very freedom, openness, and pluralism of American life make the traditional pattern [of religion] hard for Americans to understand. For one thing, the traditional pattern assumes a certain priority of the religious community over the individual. . . . For Americans, the traditional relationship between the individual and the religious community is to some degree reversed."
—Robert Bellah[5]

CHURCH SENSITIVITY

Most people either believe that churches are doing very well (35 percent) or pretty well (35 percent) at serving the needs of the people. One-sixth (17 percent) say churches are only fair at this. Very few people submit that churches are doing not too well (2 percent) or poorly (1 percent). 7

There has been a significant movement in recent years for churches to become more relevant in the eyes of those in the pews. Some progress is being made in the impression that churches are more in touch with contemporary realities. In 1991, 28 percent strongly agreed that the Christian churches in their area were relevant "to the way you live today." That figure had risen to 34 percent in 1993. The majority of adults, however, are unconvinced. 7, 14

Increasing numbers of churches are striving to be sensitive to the needs of "seekers": individuals who are not Christians but are seeking spiritual moorings and connections. Currently, 4 percent of all churches have "seeker-driven" services; 22 percent have "seeker-sensitive" services. 26

Commentary

Sensitivity and relevance are not hallmarks of the local church. For many who attend, these characteristics, when present, are viewed as a bonus, rather than maintained as a requirement. The view is quite different, however, among those who do not attend churches. Millions of them have rejected churches because of their perceived lack of relevance and sensitivity of churches to human need.

"There are thousands of local churches in the United States, representing an enormous range of variation in doctrine and worship. Yet most define themselves as communities of personal support. . . . The salience of these needs for personal intimacy in American religious life suggests why the local church, like other voluntary communities, is so fragile, requires so much energy to keep it going, and has so faint a hold on commitment when such needs are not met."
—Robert Bellah[6]

EVALUATION OF WORSHIP EXPERIENCES

Most Americans perceive the primary purpose of the local church to be the provision of a time, place, and opportunity for worship. Two-thirds of church-going adults (65 percent) are very satisfied with the ability to worship God afforded by their church.[5]

Enjoying or appreciating worship is not synonymous with experiencing the presence of God. Seven out of ten adults (71 percent) say they have never experienced God's presence at a church service. Others have had that experience: 12 percent say it "always" happens, 5 percent say it "usually" occurs, and 8 percent say it happens "sometimes."[5]

Most people have complimentary things to say about the worship services at their church. The terms most commonly selected from a list of one dozen terms offered were inspiring (92 percent); refreshing (90 percent); Spirit-filled (86 percent); participatory (82 percent); and traditional (78 percent).[5]

There is a gap in the meaning of "modern or contemporary worship" between the views of pastors and the congregation. When asked about the style of worship service offered at their church, only one out of four pastors said they had a contemporary style service. However, seven out of ten church attenders (71 percent) described their church as engaging in "modern or contemporary worship." 5

A substantial proportion of people say their church provides worship experiences which are challenging (67 percent) and life transforming (59 percent). 5

Terms which are rarely used by the public to describe their worship activities at church include embarrassing (3 percent); disappointing (7 percent); boring (12 percent); just a performance (13 percent); and outdated (13 percent). 5

There are major differences in perspective between Protestants and Catholics related to their worship experience. For instance, Protestants are more likely to say their worship experience is challenging (78 percent versus 50 percent among Catholics); life transforming (67 percent and 42 percent, respectively); and Spirit-filled (91 percent compared to 74 percent). Catholics, on the other hand, are more likely to cite their worship services as boring (19 percent versus 9 percent, respectively) and outdated (25 percent of Catholics, 6 percent of Protestants). 5

Commentary

People expect to worship at their church, and they generally feel good about their worship experience. What makes this surprising is that most congregants admit to rarely, if ever, experiencing God's presence

51

during their corporate worship time. It seems that contemporary church-goers have redefined worship from activities done in the presence of God to those acts of service, humility, and praise which are done for the benefit of God—however distant He may be from them.

Few People Expect to Change Churches

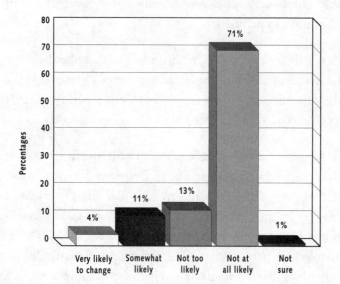

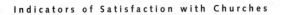

It Is Unusual to Experience God's Presence at a Church Worship Service

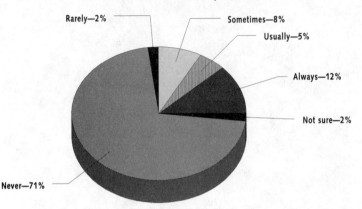

Rarely—2%

Sometimes—8%

Usually—5%

Always—12%

Not sure—2%

Never—71%

Protestants and Catholics Have Some Different Views of Their Church-based Worship Experiences

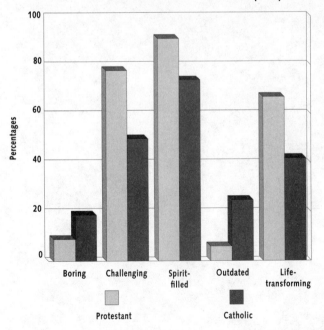

Percentages

Boring   Challenging   Spirit-filled   Outdated   Life-transforming

Protestant   Catholic

6

INVOLVEMENT WITH SACRED LITERATURE

Almost every household in America (92 percent) owns at least one copy of the Christian Bible. This includes most homes in which the adults are not practicing Christians as well as the homes of hundreds of thousands of atheists. 7

Among households which own a Bible, the typical count is three Bibles per household. 7

The proportion of adults who read from the Bible during the course of a week, other than when they are in church services, has declined dramatically since the early nineties. In 1992, nearly half of all adults (47 percent) read from the Bible during the week. That figure has plummeted to just 34 percent by 1996. The majority of the decline is attributable to a drop in Bible reading among Protestants. Their involvement with Scripture has gone from 62 percent in 1991 to 48 percent in 1996. Bible reading among Catholics has fallen from 31 percent to 21 percent during that same period.

Throughout the past decade, the pattern of Bible reading has remained consistent: Protestants are twice as likely as Catholics to read from the Bible during a given week.

The typical adult who reads from the Bible during the week will read from it on three days. That is a slight increase, from two days per week, in 1988. Overall, 26 percent read the Bible once a week, other than at a church service; 20 percent will read from it twice; 12 percent, three times; 20 percent, from four to six days; and 22 percent read the Bible every day of the week. 8, 17

Although fewer people are reading the Bible these days, those who read it spend almost one-and-a-half hours per week ingesting the Bible. 14, 17

Slightly more than half of the Protestant adults who read from the Bible during the week read along with other members of their households (57 percent). Catholics were less likely to read the Bible together (35 percent of those who had read the Bible in a given week had also read it at least once with other household members). Overall, 24 percent of all Protestants had a family Bible reading time, compared to just 7 percent among Catholics. 4

Two percent of Americans read from the Book of Mormon in a typical week. While roughly 2 percent of the adult population is Mormon, the data suggest that many Mormons do not read from this book, while tens of thousands of individuals who do not call themselves Mormon do read from it. 8

Fewer than one-half of one percent of the population reads from a sacred text of a non-Christian religion during a typical week: the I Ching, the Koran, the Torah, or the Bhagvadghita.

Commentary

The combination of declining literacy, less involvement in church-driven activities, deteriorating levels of confidence in the Christian faith, and increasing self-reliance have conspired to erode Bible reading levels. This has happened during a period when Bible publishers have spent tens of millions of dollars developing versions which are written for people who are less literate in the English language: complete Bible translations are now available for people who read at a third-grade reading level. However, Americans are not replacing the Bible with other sacred books, such as the I Ching, the Book of Mormon, or the Koran. Less than 4 percent of the population read any of the "alternative" sacred texts, combined, in a given week. The issue is not one of inadequate choices. The obstacle is convincing potential readers that the Bible—or any sacred text—has such compelling information that it is worth the time invested in such study.

"Americans revere the Bible—but, by and large, they don't read it. And because they don't read it, they have become a nation of biblical illiterates."
—George Gallup, Jr. [1]

GIVING RESOURCES

Volunteering time to a church has declined slightly since the onset of the nineties. In 1991, 27 percent of all adults said they had devoted some free time to helping out at a church during the week. That figure was down to 21 percent by 1996. The decline was more prolific among Protestants (from 35 percent to 27 percent) than Catholics (from 19 percent to 16 percent) during that time frame. 1A, 14

During a typical month, one-third of all Americans (33 percent) claim to volunteer some time to the work of their church or religious center. That represents nearly half of all people who attend a church service during the course of a month. Protestants were twice as likely as Catholics to help out (43 percent versus 22 percent, respectively). One out of four people associated with non-Christian faith groups served as volunteers during a typical month. 4

Fund-raising sources report that religious organizations, including churches and other religious groups, raise four times more money than the next most popular type of cause. Overall, slightly more than one out of seven adults give money to some type of Christian ministry, other than a church, during a typical year. The proportion of Protestants and Catholics who give to such entities is the same (about one out of three). 1A

Six out of ten adults (60 percent) claim that they have volunteered time or money within the past month to help needy people in their geographic area. In contrast, one out of four (24 percent) say they have volunteered their time or money during the prior month to help needy people who live in other countries. 11

Commentary

There is a clear behavioral pattern. Those who volunteer their time are also more consistent and more generous donors than non-volunteers. Donors, while not as committed as volunteers, are generally more deeply committed to the organizations and causes which they fund than are non-donors. People who neither participate physically nor financially in the work of a ministry are the least loyal of all.

"Americans give more money and donate more time to religious bodies and religiously associated organizations than to all other voluntary associations put together."
—Robert Bellah[2]

RELIGIOUS MEDIA

A substantial majority of the adult population has exposure to one or more forms of religious media during a typical month.

In a typical week, about one out of four adults is exposed to each of five major types of Christian media: television (24 percent); religious teaching or preaching on the radio (27 percent); Christian music on the radio (22 percent); Christian books, other than the Bible (27 percent); and Christian magazines (22 percent). [2, 5]

In a typical month, more than two-thirds of all adults have some contact with Christian media. The most common forms include television (49 percent have watched Christian programming in an average month); Christian music on the radio (45 percent); Christian teaching or preaching on the radio (39 percent); a

Christian magazine (38 percent); or a Christian book, other than the Bible (34 percent). 11

Protestants are twice as likely as Catholics to watch Christian TV. In a typical week, 30 percent of Protestants watch; 15 percent of Catholics do so. 2

Protestants are more than twice as likely as Catholics to listen to Christian radio programming. While 36 percent of Protestants listen to teaching programs in a typical week, 15 percent of Catholics do so. Almost three out of ten Protestants (28 percent) listen to Christian music on the radio during the week, versus only one out of ten Catholics (10 percent). 5

The gap between Protestants and Catholics is less sizable regarding exposure to Christian literature. One-third of Protestant adults (32 percent) read a Christian book during a typical week, compared to one-quarter (22 percent) of Catholics. Protestants are also more likely to read a Christian periodical during a typical week (30 percent) than are Catholics (20 percent). 5

The Christian media are not reserved exclusively for use by born-again Christians. A majority of the non-born-again population use Christian media each month. For instance, among the non-born-again adults, 40 percent watch Christian TV; 33 percent listen to stations which play only Christian music; 28 percent read Christian magazines; 28 percent listen to Christian preaching and teaching on the radio; and 22 percent read Christian books other than the Bible. 11

Commentary

Unexpectedly high numbers of people claim they have exposure to Christian media during the week. One must be careful in taking these reports at face value. We also discovered that the most popular "Christian" magazine is *Reader's Digest*, which adults classify as Christian because of its wholesome values and upbeat tone. Many individuals have characterized radio programs such as "The Paul Harvey Report" and "Rush Limbaugh—Live!" as "Christian" programs. Even after accounting for these skewed definitions of "Christian" media, the fact remains: millions of people engage the Christian media every day.

PRAYER AND REFLECTION

Prayer is probably the religious activity in which people most consistently engage. Nine out of ten adults (89 percent) say they pray to God. Almost eight out of ten (78 percent) pray during a typical week. 8, 4

Protestants are more likely to pray during a typical week than are Catholics by an 87 percent to 75 percent margin. 4

Most people who pray offer their prayers several times a day (52 percent). About one out of three people say they pray once a day (37 percent) when they pray. The remainder say their prayer frequency depends on the day and their circumstances. 8

The average prayer lasts just under five minutes. 8

One out of five adults (21 percent) has a time of extended prayer with members of their household during the course of the typical week. This is twice as likely among Protestants (25 percent) as among Catholics (13 percent). 4

During a typical month, one out of three adults (33 percent) participates in a group or special meeting whose primary purpose is to pray. 4

People pray about many things. A majority of adults indicate that they generally thank God for what He has done in their lives (95 percent); ask for His forgiveness for specific sins (76 percent); acknowledge His unique and superior attributes (67 percent); and ask for specific needs or desires to be met (61 percent). It is less common for people to be silent during prayer times to listen for God's response (47 percent do so). 4

Commentary

Prayer appears to be the most frequent and widely-embraced religious activity in America. Although many people do not have a clear understanding about God, nor do they necessarily believe that their prayers will be answered, they have enough hope in the power of prayer to communicate with their deity in that manner. Surprisingly few adults ever pray with another human being—family, friends, church members. Prayer remains an intensely private experience for most people.

"God is alive and very well. But right now, in America, fewer people are listening to what God has to say than ever before."

—James Patterson and Peter Kim[3]

"Prayer is a more widely practiced activity than sex, yet far more is known about the sexual practices of Americans than about their prayer lives!"
—George Gallup, Jr. and Margaret Poloma[4]

"A prayer movement that greatly surpasses anything like it in living memory, perhaps in all of Christian history, is rapidly gaining momentum. The hunger for prayer knows no denominational boundaries."
—C. Peter Wagner[5]

OTHER FORMS OF RELIGIOUS EXPRESSION

A large number of adults—24 percent— meditate during a typical month. While this practice is often associated with Eastern religions, among the people most likely to practice this activity are Protestant adults: 28 percent meditate during a typical month. Only one out of five non-Christians (19 percent) meditate at least once a month. 4

Fasting for religious reasons is undertaken by about one out of every twelve people (8 percent) each month. This is equally likely among Christians and non-Christians. 4

Six percent of adults engage in chanting during a normal month. Non-Christians are twice as likely as Christians to chant. However, 4 percent of those who attend Protestant and Catholic churches claim they chant. 4

Yoga has fallen out of use. Currently, only 2 percent of all adults do yoga. Most of those who engage in yoga are not Christian. 4

Commentary

In a turbulent society, people are open to various expressions of their faith and a greater variety of spiritual inputs than when things are calm and satisfying.

"America is far more pluralistic today than it has ever been in the past, and the patterns of religious affiliation among teenagers indicate that it is going to become even more pluralistic over the next generation."
—George Gallup, Jr. 6

SPIRITUAL COUNSEL

In a typical month, one out of three adults (36 percent) read their horoscope. This is equally common among Christians and non-Christians, Protestants and Catholics. 4

Only 3 percent of all adults consult a medium or a spiritual adviser, other than a church minister, in a typical month. Perhaps surprisingly, this behavior, too, is equally likely among Christians and non-Christians. 4

EVANGELISM AND DISCIPLESHIP

Proselytizing remains a surprisingly widespread practice in

America. During the past year, one out of three adults (32 percent) have shared their religious beliefs with someone who had different beliefs than their own. Such evangelizing was undertaken by four out of ten Protestants, one out of four Catholics, and one out of three non-Christians. 22

Among adults who engaged in evangelism at any time in the past, 25 percent of born-again Christians and 11 percent of non-Christians have found that at least one of the people they have shared their religious beliefs with converted to the evangelizer's faith. 10

The process of discipleship, in which a person who is more mature or experienced in that faith regularly mentors the newer believer about their faith, is quite common. Currently, one out of three adults (31 percent) claim they are being discipled by someone. 10

There are more students than mentors currently active in the discipling process. One-quarter of all adults (24 percent) have served as a mentor or discipler to one or more people during the past year. 10

Commentary

Evangelism may not have a positive image in the nation, but more than sixty million adults each year confront other people with their religious beliefs. And while only about one-tenth of the population serves in a formal teaching capacity at a religious center, the most common form of teaching may be through informal mentoring relationships that involve up to one-fourth of all Christians.

"Privatized faith is common among Boomers, as it is for most Americans. A history of separation of church and state, a pluralistic religious order, a heritage emphasizing personal autonomy and voluntarism, and a consumer culture have all encouraged a deeply personal type of religion."
—Wade Clark Roof [7]

CHURCH LEADERSHIP

Fewer adults are assuming positions of leadership in their church these days. In 1988, 14 percent of adults held a leadership post. By 1993, that figure had dropped to 9 percent. [8, 17]

Roughly one out of ten adults is currently involved teaching a Sunday school class, a catechism class, or another type of Christian education class at their religious center. This has remained relatively constant over the past decade.

Commentary

One of the oddities about American participation is that we do not get involved because it is the "right thing to do." More often, people get involved because they believe they can make a positive difference; they can utilize their talents and abilities to mutual benefit; or because they are responding to an urgent need which they are recruited to address. In many churches these days, none of those criteria are evident and, consequently, people choose to put their creative energies elsewhere.

"Americans have a clear sense of what they want from their churches

and synagogues, because they see religious institutions as serving people, not the people serving the institutions. One thing that millions of Americans clearly want from their churches is more influence from the laity, the people in the pews."
—George Gallup, Jr. [8]

RESPONSES TO CHURCH MARKETING

Most Americans (57 percent) have received a brochure, flyer, letter, or other piece of mail from a Christian church they have never attended, inviting them to attend that church. Of those, 10 percent eventually attended the church from which they received the printed materials. [8]

PRIORITIES

The vast majority of adults (70 percent) contend that they "consistently allow [their] lives to be guided by the Holy Spirit." [4]

When asked to identify the single most important responsibility of a Christian, the replies of born-again adults show that worship is the top-rated priority (listed by 34 percent); developing relationships with other Christians was named by 25 percent; evangelism ranked third (11 percent); seeking social justice was close behind (9 percent). [4]

Bible Reading During a Typical Week Has Declined Rapidly in the Nineties

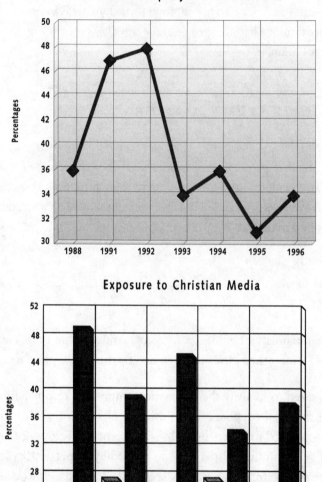

Exposure to Christian Media

In a Typical Week

In a Typical Month

Most Important Spiritual Priority
(according to born-again Christians)

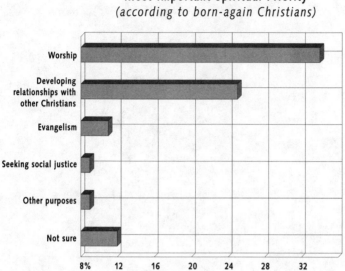

7

INDICATORS OF IMMORTALITY

PERSPECTIVES ON SPIRITUAL SALVATION

Few Americans doubt that God will judge every individual. Almost nine out of ten people (86 percent) contend that "eventually, all people will be judged by God." 8

Most Americans believe that spiritual salvation is an outcome to be earned through their good character or behavior. Six out of ten people (57 percent) believe that "if a person is generally good, or does enough good things for others during their lives, they will earn a place in heaven." This perspective has remained constant throughout the nineties. 2

Adults are evenly divided on the role played by religious beliefs in people's life-after-death experience. Forty-five percent contend that one's religious beliefs will impact their spiritual condition; another 45 percent argue that a person's beliefs will not matter. The other 10 percent refuse to take a position. 4

Commentary

The American penchant for self-reliance, achievement, and autonomy has invaded the realm of the afterlife. People are more likely to count on their own abilities and character as a means to pleasing God or otherwise earning eternal peace than they are to accept a gift—even a spiritual gift—as taught by the Christian Church regarding the sacrificial death and subsequent atonement through Jesus Christ.

"For most Americans, God is not to be feared or, for that matter, loved."
—James Patterson and Peter Kim[1]

THE ROLE OF JESUS CHRIST IN SALVATION

Three-fourths of all adults (74 percent) believe that the "forgiveness of sins is possible only through faith in Jesus Christ."[4]

Only four out of ten Americans (39 percent) believe that "people who do not consciously accept Jesus Christ as their savior will be condemned to hell."[4]

There is a growing tendency to believe that "all good people, whether or not they consider Jesus Christ to be their savior, will live in heaven after they die on earth." The public is now evenly divided on this matter: 46 percent agree, 47 percent disagree. This represents a significant change since 1992, when 40 percent agreed with this notion. [4, 11]

Commentary

Americans have managed, intellectually, to separate the concepts of forgiveness of sins—which they believe is possible only through the cleansing work of Christ—and the reception of eternal salvation—which they do not believe to be dependent upon the atonement of Christ.

"BORN-AGAIN" CHRISTIANS

If a "born-again Christian" is defined as an individual who has made a "personal commitment to Jesus Christ" that remains important in their life, and one who also believes that he or she will have eternal salvation because they have "confessed their sins and accepted Jesus Christ as their savior," then one-third of the adult public is born again. 1

Although churches in the U.S. have spent more than $530 billion dollars on ministry activities since 1980, the proportion of adults who are born again has remained virtually the same during the last fifteen years.

Most of the people who accept Jesus Christ as their savior do so at a young age. The median is age sixteen. In total, six out of ten people say they made their decision to accept Christ before age eighteen. At the other end of the age spectrum, only 8 percent of the population who are fifty or older claim to have made a decision to embrace Christ as their savior after their fiftieth birthday. 4

While evangelistic preaching receives much attention as a primary means of leading people to faith in Christ, among people who have accepted Christ as their savior, preaching is infrequently mentioned as the precipitant. The single most important factor identified by Christians in their decision were family conversations or upbringing (mentioned by 38 percent); response to a sermon (14 percent); and a conversation about Christ and eternity with a friend (10 percent). 1

Church attendance and being a born-again Christian are not one and the same. Currently, about six out of ten people (62 percent) who attend Christian churches on any given weekend are "born again." 1A This is an increase from several years ago, when 54 percent of those in attendance were not "born again." 15 The difference is attributable to the less spiritually committed adults dropping out of church activity altogether.

Commentary

There is much confusion and misinformation about born-again Christians. Sermons may play an important role in an individual's decision to follow Christ, but those sermons are rarely the most important element in the individual's choice. Most evangelistic activity . is geared at reaching adults, yet most of the people who accept Christ as savior do so during their youth.

While the media have sometimes portrayed America as a nation overrun with growing legions of born-agains, the data suggest that the size of the born-again community remains amazingly stable—in spite of enormous evangelistic spending and effort. And even though most Christian churches gear their corporate activities to believers, the data indicate that an incredibly high proportion of the people in the pews are not born again.

HELL

Only three out of ten adults (31 percent) believe that hell is a physical place of torment. Four out of ten (37 percent) describe it as a state of permanent spiritual separation from God; two out of ten (21 percent) view it merely as a symbolic term. 1

Most People Believe That "Good People" Will Earn a Place in Heaven

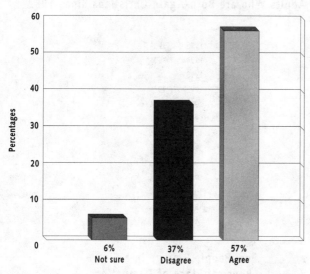

6%	37%	57%
Not sure	Disagree	Agree

People Most Often Become Christians Because of Family Members

Conversation with family member	24 %
Was raised by family to be a Christian	14 %
Responded to a sermon at a church	14 %
Conversation with a friend	10 %
Was healed of a physical problem	6 %
Attended an evangelistic event	5 %
Relationship with a minister	5 %
Death of a family member or friend	4 %
A Sunday school class or Bible study class	4 %
Experience at a youth camp or youth event	4 %
Watched an evangelistic TV program	3 %
Read the Bible	3 %
Birth of a child	2 %
Twelve-step group	1 %

There Has Been Little, If Any, Growth in the Proportion of Adults Who are Born-Again Christians Since 1982

1995	35 %
1994	35 %
1993	36 %
1992	40 %
1991	35 %
1990	34 %
1989	34 %
1988	32 %
1987	33 %
1986	34 %
1985	35 %
1982	32 %

Few People Believe in a Fiery, Physical Place of Damnation

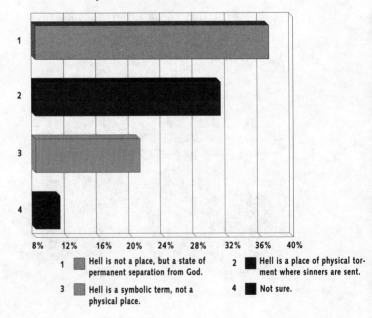

1 Hell is not a place, but a state of permanent separation from God.

2 Hell is a place of physical torment where sinners are sent.

3 Hell is a symbolic term, not a physical place.

4 Not sure.

76

8

INDICATORS OF RELIGIOUS KNOWLEDGE

UNDERSTANDING TERMINOLOGY

A common term used by church leaders is "the Great Commission." Most adults (84 percent) could not even hazard a guess as to what that term refers to. Only 9 percent of all adults were able to correctly identify it as the command given by Jesus Christ to His followers to evangelize the world. Even among born-again Christians, 80 percent did not offer a guess as to the meaning; just 14 percent provided an accurate answer. 5

The most commonly used verse of the Bible in evangelistic conversations and preaching is John 3:16. Two-thirds of the population (63 percent) has no idea what "John 3:16" refers to, much less has the ability to quote that verse. One-fifth of adults (24 percent) knew that it is a verse from the Bible that addresses salvation. Among born-again Christians, 50 percent were aware of this. 5

One of the most frequently used phrases in Christian circles is "the gospel." Amazingly, few adults know what this term means. It could either refer to its literal translation, "Good News," or to the perspective that salvation is available only through the sacrificial death and subsequent resurrection of Jesus Christ and a person's acceptance of Christ as their savior. Less than four out of ten adults (37 percent) knew this; 34 percent had other, inaccurate perceptions of the meaning of the term; three out of ten adults did not offer a guess. Even among born-again Christians, only 60 percent correctly identified at least one meaning of this expression. 5

The media often use the term "evangelical" to describe a group of religious people. Like the media, however, there is general confusion as to the meaning of this term. Only one in five adults (18 percent) correctly described the term to mean a group of Christians who are committed to evangelism and to the authority of the Bible. Just as many people had erroneous perceptions of its meaning (16 percent). Two-thirds of all Americans admitted that they had no idea what this term means. 5

Commentary

Many terms pertaining to Christianity are bandied about as if their meaning is clear and widespread. The evidence indicates otherwise. In a nation where the Christian faith is losing its grip on the public, relying upon traditional terms to summarize concepts and convey meaning is an ill-advised communication strategy. These terms are more likely to create confusion and misunderstanding than to convey substance.

UNDERSTANDING OF KEY CONCEPTS

The term "worship" means many things to many people. There is no single interpretation of the word which is common to more than one out of five people. The most likely definitions held by people related to expressions of praise or thanks to God (19 percent); praying to God (17 percent); attending church services (17 percent); having a personal relationship with God (12 percent); a particular attitude toward God (10 percent); and a way of living that reflects one's spiritual commitment (9 percent). The views of born-again Christians were not significantly different from those of other adults. 5

BIBLE KNOWLEDGE: OLD TESTAMENT

Two-thirds of adults (69 percent) are aware that the Bible describes Satan, or the devil, as an angel who formerly served God in heaven. 4

Almost two out of three adults (62 percent) know that the Book of Isaiah is in the Old Testament. One out of ten people (11 percent) believe it is in the New Testament. One out of four (27 percent) don't know. 4

Only half of all adults (49 percent) are aware that the Book of Jonah is part of the Bible. 17

Ten percent of adults believe that the name of Noah's wife was Joan of Arc. (The Bible does not provide her name.) 4

BIBLE KNOWLEDGE: NEW TESTAMENT

One out of four people (22 percent) believe that Jesus Christ never got married because He was a priest and priests did not marry. 4

One out of six people (16 percent) believe that one of the books in the New Testament is the Book of Thomas, written by the apostle Thomas. Another one-third of the population are not sure whether or not there is such a book in the New Testament of the Bible. 4

Half of all adults (49 percent) believe that the Bible teaches that "money is the root of all evil." One-third (37 percent) disagree with this contention. The actual teaching indicates that it is the love of money that is the root of all evil. 4

Two out of every three adults (68 percent) can correctly identify the number of Jesus' apostles as being twelve. 17

Almost six out of ten people (59 percent) are able to identify Bethlehem as the town in which Jesus was born. 17

Four out of five people (80 percent) incorrectly believe that the Bible includes the statement that "God helps those who help themselves." 1A

Commentary

The Bible knowledge of Americans is an unpredictable potpourri of information. In some areas we are rather astute; in others, embarrassingly ignorant. This condition is attributable to Christian education processes which are asystematic, and which incorporate little in the way of knowledge assessment.

How Americans Define "Worship"

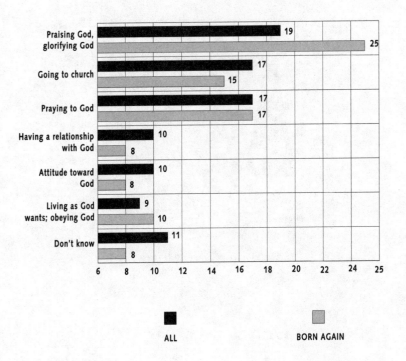

Most People Are Ignorant of the Meaning of Popular Christian Terminology

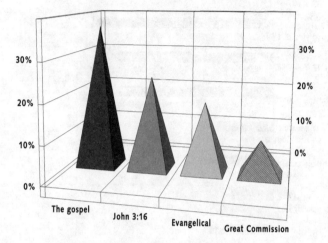

*Percentage who could correctly define these terms.

9

GENERATIONAL DIFFERENCES

For each of the following factors, there is a clear pattern: the older the person, the more likely they are to be described by the characteristic:

- have read the Bible in the past week;
- have attended church in the past week;
- have attended a church-based religious education class in the past week;
- have volunteered at a church in the past week;
- consider themselves "religious";
- say they are "absolutely committed" to the Christian faith;
- believe they have a personal responsibility to share their faith;
- say their religious faith is very important in their life;
- aware that the Bible teaches Satan was one of God's angels;
- believe that hell is a literal place where physical torment happens.

Regarding the thirty factors tested, there were only four on which there is no discernible difference between the four adult generations. Similar proportions of people from each generation strongly believe that the Bible is totally accurate in all that it teaches; believe that Satan is a symbol of evil, not a living spiritual entity; maintain that if a person is good, or does enough good things for other people during his/her life, they will earn a place in heaven; and believe that no single religious faith has all the answers to leading a successful life.

Statistically, the largest differences between the generations include these:

- Seniors (i.e., those born 1926 or earlier) are much more likely than any other group to describe themselves as "religious"; feel "absolutely committed" to the Christian faith; reject the notion that Jesus Christ sinned during His time on earth; describe God in orthodox, biblical terms; and to disagree strongly that the Bible teaches that "money is the root of all evil."

- Busters (those born between 1965 and 1983) are significantly less likely than older adults to attend church in any given week; say they are "absolutely committed" to the Christian faith; meet the "born-again" criteria; strongly agree that the Bible can be taken literally; accept the notion that people who do not accept Jesus Christ as their Savior will be condemned to hell; and to know that Jesus Christ is of the lineage of King David.

- Busters are more likely than older people to believe that all people pray to the same gods, no matter what name they assign to the spirits they pray to; and are much more likely than older adults to read their horoscope.

The three younger generations—i.e., Busters, Boomers (those born 1946 to 1964), and Builders (those born 1927–1945)—are essentially similar to each other, but significantly different from the Seniors generation, in relation to:

- saying they firmly believe the Bible is totally accurate in all that it teaches (the younger adults are less likely to embrace this perspective);

- being a formal member of a church (Seniors are much more likely to be members);

- claiming that they have a personal responsibility to share their faith with non-believers (the younger adults are not as likely to accept this as their duty);

- knowing that Satan's origins were as an angel who fell from God's favor (Seniors are much more likely to hold this view).

Commentary

The consistent differences in behavior between Busters, Boomers, Builders, and Seniors may be attributed to one of three primary reasons: an increase in traditional Christian-based religiosity as the individual ages; a steady and progressive deterioration of people's involvement in religious thought and practice, of any kind; or people retaining their personal religious fervor, but expressing that focus in ways which are radically different from the past. The most likely reality is that all three of these explanations describe part of the change that is redefining religion in America.

"For centuries it was assumed that faith was something given,

constant, unchanging. Now, however, it is clear that people go through "passages" in their spiritual lives just as they do in other dimensions of their lives. . . . Most Americans have experienced a change in their faith life. . . . Specific life experiences such as childbirth, divorce, or the death of a loved one often, but not always, trigger a change in faith."
—George Gallup, Jr.[1]

"Dropping out of organized religion during the young adult years, at least for a transitory period in a person's life, is a deeply embedded cultural pattern in America. . . . What is really significant religiously is not that they drift away, but whether or not they return to these institutions later in their lives. . . ."
—Wade Clark Roof[2]

"Greater numbers of young Americans adhere to what is described as the 'new voluntarism': church is a matter of choice, less a socially ascribed or cultural expectation."
—Wade Clark Roof[3]

GENDER DIFFERENCES

On about half of the indicators tested, women scored more "religious" than did men. Of the thirty factors examined, women had opinions or behaviors which positioned them as the more spiritual gender for thirteen factors; men and women were about equal for sixteen factors; and men outscored women on only one item.

The factors on which women score higher than men include:

- reading the Bible during the week;
- describing themselves as "religious";

- indicating that they are "absolutely committed" to the Christian faith;
- strongly asserting that the Bible is totally accurate in all it teaches;
- strongly affirming the importance of their religious faith in their life;
- strongly disagreeing that Christ sinned while He was on earth;
- choosing an orthodox, biblical description of their God;
- meeting the born-again criteria;
- reading their horoscope in a typical month;
- strongly agreeing that the Bible can be taken literally;
- believing that if a person does not consciously accept Christ as their savior, he will be condemned to hell;
- contending that the Bible teaches that "money is the root of all evil."

Men are more likely to agree that it is possible to lead a satisfying life without a spiritual focus.

Among the factors for which there is no discernible difference between men and women are volunteerism, accepting evangelistic responsibility, and most indicators of Bible knowledge.

There are three factors on which women are substantially different from men. Women are twice as likely as men to attend a church service during any given week. Women are also 50 percent more likely than men to say they are "religious" and to state that they are "absolutely committed" to the Christian faith.

Commentary

The foundation of the Christian faith in America is women. If their commitment to Christianity continues to slip, then so will the health and vitality of Christianity in America. Men seem convinced that it is the tangible realities of life, rather than spirituality, which influence a person's joy, success, and legacy.

EDUCATIONAL ACHIEVEMENT

Educational achievement has only a moderate impact on the religious lives of people. On most measures of religious behavior, knowledge, or belief, adults are similar, regardless of their educational background. Overall, those who possess a college degree are more likely to lack a traditional Christian perspective.

Just one out of five adults are college graduates. College graduates are more likely than those adults who do not have a college degree to volunteer at a church in any given week; to describe themselves as "absolutely committed" to the Christian faith; to strongly agree that there is no single religious faith which has all the answers to leading a successful life; and to know that David was related to Jesus Christ.

Adults who have not graduated from college are more likely to:

- strongly agree that the Bible is totally accurate in all it teaches;
- acknowledge a personal responsibility to evangelize;

- possess an orthodox, biblical view of God;
- believe that hell is a physical place where torment occurs;
- read their horoscope during the month;
- believe that the Bible can be taken literally;
- contend that people who do not consciously accept Christ as their savior will be condemned to hell;
- believe that the Bible teaches that money is the root of all evil.

Educational achievement has no relationship with the frequency of church attendance, the frequency of Bible reading, the likelihood of being a born-again Christian, or upon depth of Bible knowledge.

While the number of differences based on education is not as great as the number of distinctions attributable to some other demographic variables, educational achievement is one of the demographic attributes most likely to produce large gaps between the segments examined.

Commentary

Critics of religion contend that it is a crutch for the disadvantaged, a sedative against the social displacement and absence of empowerment they endure. The evidence, however, does not bear out such a conclusion. Religion is just as significant—or insignificant—to the well-educated as to the less educated. Faith remains a core part of the existence of most Americans—a declining core element, perhaps, but still sufficiently significant—that most people acknowledge and, in some ways, pursue their spiritual development.

REGIONAL DIFFERENCES

There are few religious factors for which there is not some type of significant distinction across regions. The general pattern is that the South emerges as the most traditionally Christian and most religious region; the Northeast and West emerge as the least Christian and least religious areas; and the Midwest rarely emerges as a leader on any religious measurement, usually falling in the middle ground between the extremes of the other three regions.

The Northeast emerges as the area most involved in and supportive of the "New Age" faith patterns. People in the Northeast were unusually likely to:

- chant;
- read their horoscope;
- believe that astrology can accurately predict the future;
- believe that everyone has the same spiritual outcome after life, no matter what faith they did or did not believe in;
- firmly contend that there is not a particular religious faith which has all the answers to leading a successful life;
- believe that Jesus Christ sinned while He was on earth;
- and to strongly argue that the entire Bible was written several decades after the death of Jesus Christ.

Residents of the Western states were least likely to read horoscopes; take the Bible literally; believe that people are condemned to hell if they do not consciously accept Christ as their savior; accept tarot cards as a reliable source of guidance; and be a member of a church.

For one-third of the factors examined, residents of the Eastern and Western states had nearly identical response levels—levels which clearly differentiated them from people in the Midwestern and Southern states. While the Northeast is clearly most comfortable with New Age faith practices and thinking, both the Northeast and West have deep-rooted difficulties with Christianity and its most fundamental perspectives. The two "power zones" (i.e. Northeast and West) were lowest on volunteering at a religious center; describing themselves as "religious;" being "absolutely committed" to Christianity; strongly agreeing that the Bible is totally accurate; firmly believing that they have a personal responsibility to evangelize; viewing religion as very important in their life; being born again; describing hell as a physical place of torment; and knowing that Jesus was related to David.

On a majority of the thirty factors compared across regions, the South rose as the segment most likely—often by whopping margins—to assume the traditional Christian position. The factors for which its supremacy was most notable included:

- citing themselves as "religious";
- being "absolutely committed" to Christianity;
- saying the Bible is totally accurate in its teaching;
- taking personal responsibility for evangelism;
- being born again;
- believing in hell as a physical place of torment;
- taking the Bible literally;
- rejecting the possibility of leading a fully satisfying life without a strong spiritual emphasis;

- concurring that unless a person embraces Christ as their savior they will be doomed to hell;

- rejecting the notion that everyone prays to the same deity, no matter what names they use for their god.

The Midwest stood out on only one variable: it has the highest proportion of church members of the four geographic regions.

Commentary

Though weakened by the changing culture, the Bible Belt remains intact. The Midwest, often thought to be the home of America's "heartland" values, which include devotion to Christianity, is not nearly as committed to Christianity as many assume. The Northeast and West have earned their reputations as the areas least friendly to Christianity, most open to New Age spirituality, and the areas in which people are least likely to accept the notion of spiritual growth as a key to human development and fulfillment.

ETHNIC GAPS

While there are many racial idiosyncrasies regarding religion, the biggest gaps are between whites and Hispanics, not whites and blacks.

Each of the three largest racial groups—whites, Hispanics, and blacks—has areas of spirituality in which they are notably divergent from the American norm. Hispanics are most likely to distance themselves from traditional Christian beliefs. Whites are most likely to have less engagement in Christian disciplines, such as Bible reading and church attendance. Blacks are the most likely to embrace the importance of religious faith and the fundamental ideology of Christianity.

Whites are lowest among the three groups when it comes to church attendance; accepting the accuracy of the Bible; engagement in evangelism; citing their religious faith as very important to them; and reading horoscopes. Although they are lowest in terms of church attendance, they are highest in terms of being a member of a church.

Blacks differed from others by being the most likely to call themselves "religious"; attend Sunday school classes; accepting the Bible's teachings as totally accurate, and that it can be taken literally; strongly agreeing that they have a personal responsibility to evangelize; and believing that astrology can predict their future. They are also the least likely group to accept the idea that a person can lead a full and satisfying life without a significant commitment to spirituality.

The Hispanic population is the most likely to describe Christ as a sinner; to believe in a physical place of torment called hell; to engage in yoga; to read their horoscope; and to believe that everyone experiences the same ultimate outcome, regardless of their religious beliefs or practices.

The Hispanic population was also significantly less likely than other adults to:

- volunteer at churches;
- say they are totally committed to Christianity;

- attend religious education classes at their religious center;
- believe that astrology provides an accurate forecast of their future;
- take the Bible literally;
- believe that you must have a spiritual side to lead a full and satisfying life;
- accept the idea that non-Christians will go to hell;
- feel that no single religious faith has all the answers to being successful in life;
- be a member of a church;
- believe that the entire Bible was written several decades after Jesus' death.

Blacks and Hispanics, together, were much more likely than whites to attend church services; read the Bible; state that their religious faith is very important in their life; and to have chanted in the past month.

The levels of acceptance of fundamental Christian theology and of biblical knowledge were amazingly similar for all three groups. There was no statistically significant difference among whites, blacks, and Hispanics regarding:

- the perspective that Satan is symbolic;
- belief that a person can earn eternal salvation;
- maintaining an orthodox, biblical definition of God;
- being born again;
- believing that everyone prays to the same deity, no matter what name they attach to their spiritual force;

- accepting tarot cards as reliable;
- not knowing that there is not a Book of Thomas in the New Testament of the Bible;
- not realizing that Jesus Christ was related to David;
- believing that the Bible teaches that money is the root of all evil.

Commentary

America's three dominant ethnic groups are vastly different when it comes to spiritual matters. (If we had sufficient data on Asians, they would undoubtedly expand the pool to *four* distinct segments.) Caucasians are largely responsible for the homogenization of Christianity. White adults have softened the most pointed and challenging themes of biblical Christianity such that the distinctives of that faith are sometimes difficult to identify. African-Americans appear to wrap themselves in the form and experience of Christianity, perhaps gaining hope from the gospel message, but giving limited evidence of life transformation in response to its moral imperatives. Hispanics, the fastest-growing of the three groups, are still working through basic cultural assimilation challenges, usually transitioning from some type of Catholic upbringing to a more world-religion perspective. As such, they are a segment whose ultimate religious leanings are yet to be determined. They seem satisfied with none of the options that lie before them.

CATHOLICS AND PROTESTANTS

Protestants and Catholics shared more similarities than might have been imagined. On one-third of the factors explored, they were indistinguishable. On those matters which they differed, however, the gaps were unusually substantial.

Catholics were more likely than Protestants to argue that spirituality is not necessary to lead a complete and satisfying life; believe that everyone prays to the same god regardless of the name associated with that deity; and that everyone experiences the same outcome after death, no matter what their religious beliefs were while they lived.

Protestants were somewhat more likely than Catholics to call themselves "religious"; cite their religious faith as very important; to strongly disagree that Christ was a sinner; possess an orthodox, biblical view of God; believe in a physical place of torment known as hell; know of Satan's origins; and know David and Christ were related.

Protestants were twice as likely as Catholics to read the Bible in a given week; volunteer at their church; claim to be absolutely committed to Christianity; firmly assert the accuracy of Bible teaching; accept personal responsibility for sharing the gospel of Christ; acknowledge that Satan is a real being; and embrace a literal interpretation of Scripture.

Protestants were three times more likely than Catholics to attend a Christian education class in any given week and to be born-again Christians.

Protestants were five times more likely than Catholics to agree that people who do not consciously accept Christ as their savior will be condemned to hell. They were eight times more likely to strongly disagree that a person can earn a place in heaven by being good or by doing good for others.

Catholics and Protestants are indistinguishable when it comes to the following:

- church attendance;
- doing yoga;
- chanting;
- reading their horoscope;
- believing in the accuracy of astrology;
- believing that tarot cards are a reliable source of guidance;
- contending that no single religious faith has all the answers to leading a fulfilling and complete life;
- being a member of a church;
- believing that there is a Book of Thomas in the New Testament;
- believing that the entire Bible was written several decades after the death of Jesus Christ;
- believing that the Bible teaches that money is the root of all evil.

Commentary

How can we explain the maintenance of significantly divergent religious practices alongside indistinguishable belief patterns other than to suggest that many Protestants and Catholics have chosen the style, rather than the substance, of Christianity? Instead of striving to define and benefit from the richness of their respective religious heritage and traditions, most adults are on religious "automatic pilot." The meaningful distinctions delineated by the Reformation have effectively been closed through the determined, readily discernible theological ignorance of Americans.

"The most recent expansion of pluralism signifies the collapse of the long-standing Judeo-Christian consensus in American public life. However much Protestants, Catholics, and Jews through the last half of the nineteenth century and the first half of the twentieth distrusted each other socially, even competed with each other economically, politically, and religiously, there remained a certain agreement about the language of public debate. . . . With the expansion of pluralism in the second half of the twentieth century, that agreement has largely disintegrated. But the significance of the trend toward expanded pluralism does not reside in this disintegration alone but rather in its consequences: in the wake of the fading Judeo-Christian consensus has come a rudimentary realignment of pluralistic diversity. The 'organizing principle' of American pluralism has altered fundamentally such that the major rift is no longer born out of theological or doctrinal disagreements—as between Protestants and Catholics or Christians and Jews. Rather the rift emerges out of a fundamental disagreement over the sources of moral truth."
—James Davison Hunter [4]

Church Attendance Varies by Background
(percentage who attended in the past week)

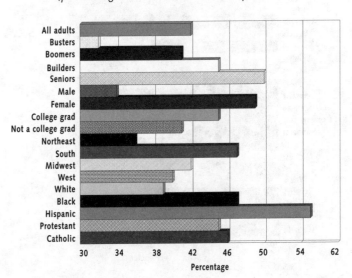

Some People Are Likely to Read the Bible; Others Are Not
(percentage who read the Bible in the past week)

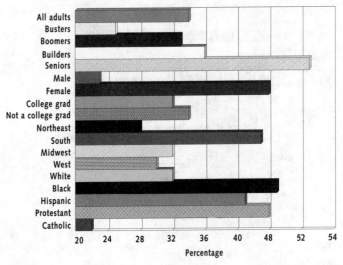

Not Many Segments of Adult America Are "Absolutely Committed" to Christianity

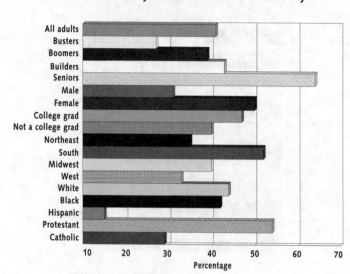

Born-Again Adults Come from All Walks of Life—and in Similar Proportions

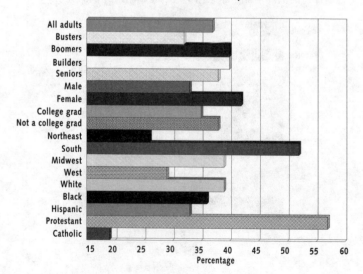

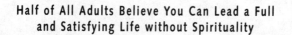

Half of All Adults Believe You Can Lead a Full and Satisfying Life without Spirituality

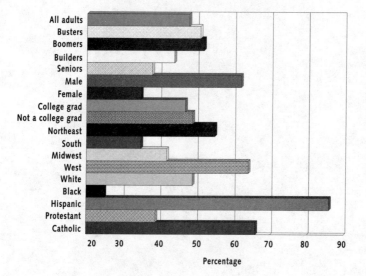

Percentage

10

INDICATORS OF RELIGIOUS INFLUENCE

RELIGION'S INFLUENCE ON LIFE VIEWS

The factors which have the greatest impact on people's views and beliefs regarding life are their religious views (mentioned by 42 percent) and the attitudes and opinions of their family and friends (32 percent). No other influences are described by even one out of ten adults as the major influence on their life views. 8

Almost half of all adults say that they either always (27 percent) or often (17 percent) consciously think of themselves as a representative of Jesus Christ. This is in contrast to the three out of ten who either always (16 percent) or often (14 percent) regard themselves as representatives of their church or synagogue. While 28 percent rarely or never think of themselves as Jesus' representatives, 43 percent rarely or never think of themselves as their church's representatives. 8

Commentary

The importance of religion in people's lives is upheld by the large proportions of adults who turn to religious beliefs to guide their life choices, and by the frequency with which they behave as intentional agents of Jesus Christ. While one may quarrel with the ways in which they represent the Christian faith or their savior, the encouraging insight is that people consciously admit religious perspectives into their daily lines of reasoning.

"While religion is highly popular in America, it is to a large extent superficial; it does not change people's lives to the degree one would expect from the level of professed faith."
—George Gallup, Jr.[1]

"For most people, religion plays virtually no role in shaping their opinions on a long list of important public questions."
—James Patterson and Peter Kim[2]

"While all these religious movements are, of course, different, and frequently clash with one another, and while some are extremist and others not, all of them—Christian or New Age, Judaic or Islamic—are united in one thing: their hostility to secularism, the philosophical base of mass democracy."
—Alvin Toffler[3]

RELIGION AS AN INFLUENCE REGARDING TRUTH AND ETHICS

One out of four Americans (23 percent) state that religious beliefs and teaching are the single, most significant influence on their thinking about whether or not there is such a thing as absolute moral truth. The next most prolific influence is said to be the Bible (15 percent). Other significant sources of influence about moral truth are family (13 percent), experience (10 percent), and emotions and intuition (7 percent). [2]

When adults make ethical or moral decisions, various influences come into play. One out of five adults (20 percent) claim that the Bible is the dominant influence on their decisions. While biblical influence is not as common as that of personal past experience (cited by 28 percent), it does surpass the influence of simply choosing among the available options and their likely outcomes (13 percent) or relying upon the conventional wisdom (12 percent). 8

Commentary

"It is impossible to have a moral community or nation without faith in God, because without it everything rapidly comes down to 'me,' and 'me' alone is meaningless. . . . Great moral societies have a common belief in something beyond themselves."
—Georgie Anne Geyer, syndicated columnist 4

"At the core of the problem, as many believers see it, is a crisis of commitment: people do not take seriously their vows, their duties, and their obligations—to others and to God."
—Wade Clark Roof 5

THE CHURCH'S INFLUENCE ON SOCIETY

According to adults, when compared to five years ago, 21 percent believe that churches now have more influence than before; 41 percent contend that the degree of influence has remained stable; and 33 percent believe that the church's influence has decreased. 10

Commentary

"If there is to be an effective public church in the Unites States today, bringing the concerns of biblical religion into the common discussion about the nature and future of our society, it will probably have to be one in which the dimensions of church, sect, and mysticism all play a significant part, the strengths of each offsetting the deficiencies of the others."
—Robert Bellah [6]

"Privatized faith is common in contemporary America because it is so very congenial with a highly differentiated society. Restricted largely to the spheres of family and personal life, it encroaches very little into the larger public world, which Americans increasingly define as off-limits to religion. What one believes in private is one's own personal matter, and hence off-limits to religious institutions. With believing disjointed from belonging, it amounts to a 'portable' faith—one that a believer can keep in the inner life and take along in life, having little contact with a religious institution or ascribed group."
—Wade Clark Roof [7]

"History teaches us that when a barbarian race confronts a sleeping culture, the barbarian always wins."
—Arnold Toynbee [8]

"We don't follow what our church says because we're not interested enough to find out what it's saying."
—James Patterson and Peter Kim [9]

Sources of Ethical and Moral Influence

1 Past experience.

2 The Bible.

3 Available choices, likely outcomes.

4 Common wisdom.

5 just let whatever happens, happen.

6 Advice of friends.

7 Combination of factors.

8 Don't know.

Religion Has Less Influence on Society
Today Than Five Years Ago

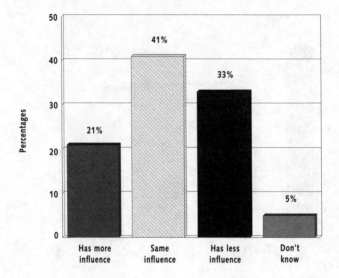

11

INDICATORS OF CHURCH STRENGTH

CHURCH ATTENDANCE FIGURES

Average attendance, by adults, at the worship services of Protestant churches has varied in the past decade. It has gone from an average of ninety-seven adults attending services during a typical weekend in 1987, up to a high of one hundred two adults in 1992, down to ninety-two in 1995. 25, 26, 27

There are approximately 310,000 Protestant churches in the U.S. Less than 2 percent of them are "mega-churches," which are widely defined as congregations which have 2,000 or more people attending their worship services each weekend. 26

Just one out of every six Protestant churches (17 percent) have two hundred or more adults attending their services on a weekend. 26

Average attendance in the mainline Protestant churches—United Methodist, Evangelical Lutheran, Episcopal, Presbyterian Church (U.S.A.), and United Church of Christ—has dropped to just ninety-eight adults. 28

Attendance at evangelical churches has slowed after a period of growth in the seventies and eighties. The average adult attendance at these churches is currently one hundred one adults. **28**

Commentary

The attention of the media has been focused on some of the peripheral elements of church attendance. The core issues are the continuing decline of attendance in mainline—or, as some now call them, sideline—churches; the tapering off of attendance growth at evangelical bodies; and the fact that most churches remain at less than one hundred people. Megachurches get an unwarranted degree of attention, given their numbers in the religious landscape, although their strategies and tactics for bringing Christianity into the modern era make them a key to understanding the future of the Christian church in America.

CHURCH REVENUE

Giving to Protestant churches has consistently increased. While the average annual revenue of a congregation was $69,213 in 1987, it has since risen to $95,513. **26, 27**

Four out of ten Protestant churches (39 percent) ask people to provide a financial pledge for the coming year—an estimated amount of money that they will donate to the church over the course of the year. Pastors of those churches estimate that, on average, about 60 percent of their congregants offer a pledge. **28**

Two-thirds of the pastors of Protestant churches (64 percent) contend that their congregations are donating less money than the amount they could reasonably be expected to contribute. Thirty percent say their congregations are giving what would be expected; 4 percent believe their congregations give beyond what might reasonably be expected from such a congregation. 28

Four out of ten Protestant churches say they currently receive money from wills, trusts, estates, and other financial legacies.[28]

About two-thirds of all adults (63 percent) give some money to a religious center during the course of the year. 24

Among those who give to a religious center, the average cumulative donation for the year amounts to less than 2 percent of their household's gross income. About 5 percent of the public tithes their income to a religious center. 1A

Commentary

Money is one of the tensions that many churches battle. Pastors feel frustrated because they dream of ministry that goes unfulfilled, simply for lack of funds—funds which they are convinced could easily be provided by their congregants. The people in the pews, meanwhile, tire of the church's pleas for money, convinced that the church is too focused on finances and not sufficiently dependent upon God's provision. The only group that seems emotionally removed from this struggle is the tithers—the one out of twenty adults who are generally at peace with giving away a double-digit share of their income.

INDICATORS OF SELF-PERCEPTION

Among Protestant churches, 78 percent consider themselves "mainline;" 75 percent "theologically conservative;" 23 percent "fundamentalist;" 13 percent "theologically liberal;" and 10 percent "pentecostal or charismatic." 26

Among the churches which are associated with an "evangelical" denomination, 62 percent described themselves as "mainline." 26

Churches that were part of the five major "mainline" denominations—United Methodist, Evangelical Lutheran, Presbyterian Church U.S.A., United Church of Christ, and Episcopal—were more than twice as likely as others to place themselves in the "theologically liberal" camp (24 percent). 26

One out of every six churches from evangelical denominations (17 percent) said they are "pentecostal or charismatic." The same was true for just 3 percent of the churches aligned with the mainline denominations. 26

Commentary

"A church that can be counted on and that can count on its members can be a great source of strength in reconstituting the social basis of our society. Such a church may also, through its social witness, have the influence to help move our society in a healthier direction. To be effective, however, the church tradition in the United States would have to be revitalized by taking seriously the criticisms of it by sectarian and mystical religion."
—Robert Bellah[1]

How Protestants Churches See Themselves

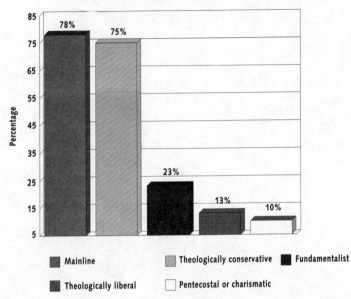

Mainline
Theologically conservative
Fundamentalist
Theologically liberal
Pentecostal or charismatic

Attendance Is Declining at the Typical Protestant Church

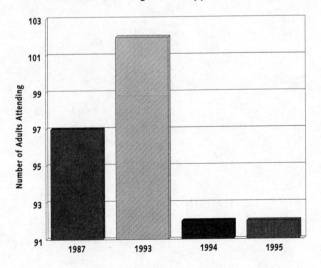

12

THE RESPONSIBILITY

In eight out of ten Protestant churches, there is only one full-time, paid staff person: the senior pastor. 28

About half of all Protestant churches (54 percent) have only one paid employee—the pastor. Among the other half, most (25 percent) have one or two part-time, paid assistants helping the pastor. 26

LEADERS' VIEWS OF THE LOCAL CHURCH

Only one out of five senior pastors of Protestant churches (21 percent) are "very satisfied" with the overall ministry of their church. The proportion expands to four out of five (82 percent) when we include those who are "somewhat satisfied." 25

When asked what Jesus Christ would say about the effectiveness of the Church if He returned to earth today, 2 percent say He would describe the Church as doing "tremendous, highly effective work;" 41 percent feel He would assess the Church as doing "a respectable, if not entirely successful job;" 41 percent believe He would characterize the Church as "showing little positive impact on souls and society;" and 3 percent state that He would criticize the Church for "failing miserably at every turn." The remaining 13 percent are evenly divided between those who give other perspectives and those who have no idea. 28

Pastors express concerns about the climate for Christianity. Just 2 percent strongly agree that "American adults are becoming more accepting of the Christian faith." 25

Only 3 percent of all pastors claim that Christian churches consistently work in cooperation with each other to achieve shared ministry goals. 25

Commentary

It must be difficult to motivate the average believer to be excited about serving Christ when the leaders themselves are lacking in enthusiasm.

LEADERS' VIEWS OF THE CONGREGATION

Two-thirds of all Protestant pastors (64 percent) believe that their church is limited financially because the congregation is giving less than its reasonable capacity. Only 4 percent said their congregation is giving beyond what could reasonably be expected. 28

Half of all pastors (49 percent) believe that churches are hindered in ministry by the lack of sufficient money. 25

Only one out of every three pastors (32 percent) say that most Christian adults are capable of effectively sharing their faith with non-believers. 25

Commentary

Pastors clearly perceive that there are two resources their congregants possess but which they refuse to part with: their money and the gospel.

LEADER SATISFACTION

Four out of ten pastors (39 percent) say they feel "very fulfilled" by their ministry efforts. The cumulative total of those who are very or somewhat satisfied reaches nine out of ten pastors (89 percent). 25

Four out of every ten pastors of Protestant churches do not believe that their present church experience is significantly enhancing their relationship with Jesus Christ. 25

Pastors are ambivalent about the influence of their ministry upon their personal passion for serving Christ. Forty-one percent are certain their passion for ministry has been increased during their current pastorate; 38 percent are somewhat persuaded of this; and 21 percent say their passion to serve God has not been increased in their present church position. 25

Pastors contend that the greatest ministry frustrations they encounter are due to the lack of commitment to ministry among the people in their congregation (listed by 30 percent); having to handle financial and administrative duties despite limited competence in those areas (13 percent); the inability to effectively reach non-believers (12 percent); and the difficulty of implementing change in the church (10 percent). On a personal level, half of all pastors (49 percent) also contend that their family life has suffered significantly as a result of the pressures and demands of their ministry. 25

In the past, young men prepared for the pastorate and, once accepted by a church, remained active in pastoral duties for an average of more than thirty years. Today, the stress, disappointments, and challenges of pastoral duties are evident in the diminished tenure of the professional clergy. On average, today's pastors last only four years at a church and the average length of a pastoral career is just fourteen years—less than half of what it was not long ago. 25

Commentary

Protestant pastors share at least one critical condition with their congregants: a struggle to grow and remain excited spiritually. In proprietary research, we have discovered that pastors are the single, most occupationally-frustrated professionals in America. Their perspectives indicate that if they sensed greater ministry impact, they would be more enthusiastic and aggressive. The population-at-large, meanwhile, needs profound, visionary, effective leadership to guide them into a deeper and more intense relationship with Christ.

THE SELF-PERCEIVED STRENGTHS OF LEADERS

One out of every four pastors claim they are excellent in the areas of scriptural knowledge (28 percent), demonstrating compassion (28 percent) and teaching/preaching (27 percent). Only one out of seven (14 percent) rate themselves similarly when it comes to providing leadership for their church. Eight percent say they are excellent managers of the others involved in the church's ministry. 25

Six percent of pastors believe they have been given the gift of leadership by God. 25

Commentary

The pastors of Protestant churches are, by their own description, teachers and preachers, rather than leaders. While there is nothing wrong with that—churches certainly require strong teaching—the typical church is not likely to grow or to maximize its impact without strong leadership to guide the ministry.

Pastors and the Laity Have Very Different Spiritual Gifts

SPIRITUAL GIFTS	PASTORS	LAITY
Teaching/preaching	52 %	7%
Administration	13 %	2%
Pastoring	12 %	*
Evangelism	9 %	2%
Mercy	8 %	4%
Exhortation/encouragement	8 %	*
Leadership	6 %	1%
Faith	4 %	4%
Counseling	4 %	1%
Prophecy	4 %	3%
Helps	2 %	7%
Knowledge	2 %	4%

Percentage of Pastors Who Believe Most Christian Adults Are Capable of Effectively Sharing their Faith with Non-Christians

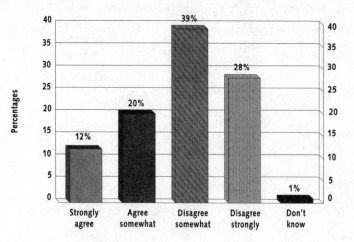

13

This chapter offers something a bit different: statistical indices of religious conditions. Each index has been developed as a means of comparing different aspects of America's spirituality to give some sense of how things have been changing on the religion scene in America over the past decade or so. Although most of these measures cover a relatively brief period of time, each index sheds some light on the religious character of the nation. While the numbers themselves are not always associated with some objective reality, the cumulative effect is to provide one more angle from which we may examine the spiritual side of America.

RELIGIOSITY INDEX

This index is based on the proportion of Americans who have engaged in any religious practice during the week. Such practices include attending religious services; attending religious education classes; praying; volunteering; contributing money to their religious center; chanting; fasting for a religious purpose; doing yoga; meditating; consulting a spiritual guide or medium; participating in a small group that meets for religious purposes; or reading holy literature.

The maximum score for this index is 1,000. Such a score would indicate that every adult is involved in at least one consistent act of personal spiritual development; consistent communication with their deity; regular involvement in corporate religious activity; and the giving of their personal resources or abilities for the good of the religious community to which they belong.

Maximum score: 1,000

    1995—310

    1994—347

    1993—307

    1992—388

    1991—399

    1988—310

    1987—264

The Religiosity Index suggests that the late eighties and early nineties were a time of comparatively hot pursuit of religious wholeness. Consistent with the individual measures we have seen throughout this book, though, religiosity began a decline in 1991, which does not yet seem to have ended.

EVANGELICAL INDEX

Using people's answers to eight questions to identify an individual as an evangelical, this index shows the change in the proportion of adults who could be defined as evangelicals. The defining attributes of evangelicals are: they assert that they have made a personal commitment to Jesus Christ that is important in their life; they say that their religious faith is very important in their life; they believe that they will have eternal life because they have confessed their sins and have accepted Christ as their savior; they have a biblical perception of God, the Father; they believe that the Bible is totally accurate in all it teaches; they acknowledge a personal responsibility to share their faith with nonbelievers; they believe that the only means to spiritual salvation is through the grace of God, provided by the death, resurrection, and ascension of Jesus Christ; they contend that Christ was both God and man, but remained untainted by sin.

Realize that evangelicals, when defined in this manner, are not synonymous with "born-again Christians," as is commonly assumed by the mass media. Instead, evangelicals are a more intensely spiritual subset of the born-again segment. Evangelicals, through this definition, may be either conservative or liberal in their political ideology, liberal or conservative in their theological leanings, and Protestant, Catholic, or unattached. Being an evangelical, technically, has nothing to do with denominational ties or church attendance.

1996—8 percent

1995—9 percent

1994—10 percent

1993—10 percent

1992—12 percent

1991—7 percent

The data underscore the fact that evangelicals are far from the monolithic political juggernaut that some portray them to be.

Until recently, the group has not been particularly cohesive as a body, although it has been relatively together ideologically. Understand, too, that this group may be growing in influence, but it does not appear to be growing numerically.

FAITH OF CHOICE INDEX

There are seven primary faiths from which Americans choose their religious focus. Those faith groups might be thought of as follows:

- *Biblical Christianity*: full acceptance of the authority of the Bible, total trust in Christ for salvation, involvement in evangelism, active participation in the life of a church, seeking continuing and more intense spiritual development, life informed by faith principles, moral absolutes exist.

- *Conventional Christianity*: total trust in Christ for their salvation, involvement in church life, appreciation for the Bible, general privatization of their faith, life only vaguely influenced by faith views, morality is relative.

- *Cultural Christianity*: universalism and works-based theology, nominal church involvement ("Christmas Christians"), non-practicing, Christian in name and (perhaps) heritage only, morality is relative.

- *New Age Practitioner*: faith as a private matter, religious principles from variety of sources, no centralized religious authority, deity intermingled with self, more focused upon religious consciousness than religious practice.

- *Jewish*: adherent of the traditional Jewish faith.
- *Atheist/Agnostic*: oblivious to the faith realm.
- *Other*: adherents to any of an amalgam of faith groups or to highly individualistic perspectives on spirituality. Among the major faith groups included would be Islam, Mormonism, Buddhism, and Hinduism.

During the course of the nineties, there has been rather remarkable stability in people's faith of choice. The most notable flux has been between Conventional and Cultural Christians, suggesting that there is a substantial degree of "softness" to the faith of many who are at the heart of church-related activity and Christian ministry.

	1995	1994	1993	1992	1991
Biblical Christianity	10%	7%	8%	9%	7%
Conventional Christianity	25	33	30	28	29
Cultural Christianity	28	21	33	21	27
New Age Practitioner	19	21	19	22	20
Jewish	1	1	1	2	2
Atheist/Agnostic	9	10	4	9	8
Other	8	7	5	9	7

SELF-EVALUATION OF SPIRITUALITY INDEX

One exercise we use occasionally is to ask people to rate themselves on a ten-point scale of personal spiritual development. The scale is described as an upright ladder with ten rungs, and the individual is asked to indicate which rung they would be standing on to indicate their spiritual development to date. The higher up the ladder, the more spiritually advanced they consider themselves to be, with rung one equal to no spiritual development and rung ten equaling maximum spiritual development.

The statistics show that there has been little change in people's self-perceived levels of spiritual maturity. Most people place themselves in the middle of the continuum. If anything, there has been slight upward movement, suggesting that a growing proportion of adults think of themselves as above average in spiritual maturity. A surprisingly high proportion of people—one out of five—place themselves on one of the top three rungs of the imaginary ladder. Ironically, the same proportion locate themselves on one of the bottom three rungs of the ladder.

Scale	1993	1986
1	5%	7%
2	4	3
3	10	9
4	12	13
5	25	33
6	14	10
7	13	10
8	10	8
9	3	2
10	5	5
median	5	5
mean	5.5	5.2

Religiosity Index

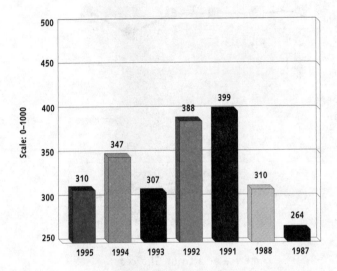

Evangelicals Are a Small Part
of the American Landscape

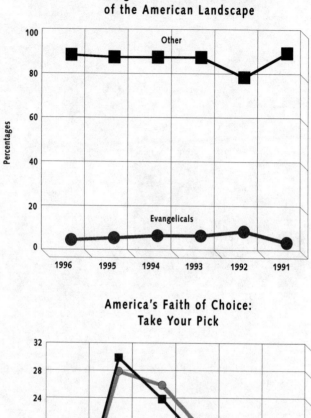

America's Faith of Choice:
Take Your Pick

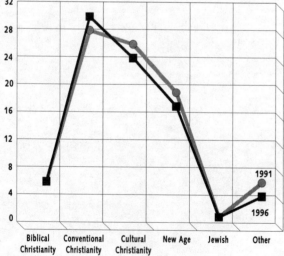

14

A SUBJECTIVE PERSPECTIVE ON
AMERICAN SPIRITUALITY

You can say many things about religion in America. It is controversial. It has become big business. It is complex. It is widely
endorsed, revered, pursued. It is diverse. But perhaps most
important of all is the recognition that religion is integral to the
American life. Unless you understand the religious character of
the nation, you cannot truly comprehend the nation.

The religious scene in America today is undergoing fundamental
changes of seismic proportions. Like almost everything in our
culture today, there is nothing sacred anymore, even in the realm
of the sacred. Americans are questioning everything about religion and faith, and the long-term taboos have been discarded in
favor of a wholesale re-evaluation. Those who dream of a nation
that will return to the readily definable, easily categorized religious landscape of the past are yearning for a reality that will
never return. We are continually evolving as a nation, and our
quest for spiritual comfort and security is one of the defining
components of the nouveau character.

While the notion threatens the serenity of many, the undeniable reality is that America is transitioning from a Christian nation to a syncretistic, spiritually diverse society. It is shifting from a denominational landscape to a domain of independent churches. It is a country where past defenses against ecumenism are giving way to the perceived benefits of cooperation, understanding, and consensus. The days of theological rigidity are history; America is now a theologically pluralistic and encompassing society.

In much the same way that the Protestant Reformation revolutionized the religious world in its day, a new reformation is redefining the spiritual heartbeat of the United States. One of the casualties in this process of development has been traditional religious terminology. Adults and youth alike reflect astounding ignorance of basic adjectives and phrases which describe what people believe, how they behave, and why they respond to religious opportunities. What is *not* lost in this spiritual upheaval is the new perception of religion: a personalized, customized form of faith views which meet personal needs, minimize rules and absolutes, and which bear little resemblance to the "pure" form of any of the world's major religions.

The religious climate in America these days reflects the true soul of the population: one which thirsts for experience rather than knowledge, for exposure rather than understanding, for choices rather than the simplicity and security of a limited set of alternatives.

Traditional measures of religious activity and belief are on the decline. But as we comprehend the religious revolution in progress, the inevitable conclusion is that some of these measures are no longer relevant in our effort to understand American religion. In an era when people do not join organizations, why should church membership be a key statistic? When religion becomes a private matter, and it is frequently practiced in unique ways outside of corporate gatherings, how important are church attendance figures as a measure of the activity of the religious community? In a nation in which functional illiteracy is one of the defining attributes, and in which technological proficiency is on the rise, does a decline in Bible reading indicate that people are less involved in Christianity? In a land where the notion of absolute truth is widely rejected, is the issue of the Bible's authority a core indicator of the spiritual pulse?

Gaining a tidy picture of the spiritual condition of America is impossible—certainly no more than it is possible to gain a tidy picture of American values, lifestyles, relational networks, and the like. What we can take away from a statistical portrait of the spiritual pulse of the nation, as provided in the preceding pages, is a vivid understanding of the significance, the diversity, and the spectrum of shades of religiosity and spirituality in the U.S. In some ways, the religious journey of the nation is predictable and mirrors the experiences of other developed, secularizing nations (e.g. Great Britain, Italy). In other ways, the path trodden by the U.S. is idiosyncratic. In the end, though, all of the evidence underscores the most crucial point of all: Americans want their religious freedom and they cherish their religious life, in all of its unique forms. Religion in this country may not be what it used to be, but indisputably it remains a vital dimension of the American experience.

NOTES

CHAPTER 1

1. Bellah, Robert, et. al., *Habits of the Heart*, (New York, NY: Harper & Row Publishers, 1985), page 226.
2. Carter, Stephen, *The Culture of Disbelief*, (New York, NY: Basic Books, 1993), page 41.
3. Kosmin, Barry and Lachman, Seymour, *One Nation Under God*, (New York, NY: Harmony Books, 1993), page 1.
4. Gallup, George H., Jr. and Castelli, Jim, *The People's Religion*, (New York, NY: Macmillan Publishing Company, 1989), page 251.
5. Kosmin and Lachman, ibid, page 279.
6. Roof, Wade Clark, *A Generation of Seekers*, (New York, NY: Harper Collins, 1993), page 245.
7. Anderson, Leith, *A Church for the 21st Century*, (Minneapolis, MN: Bethany House Publishers, 1992), page 19.
8. Roof, ibid, pages 156–159.
7. Bellah et. al., ibid, page 247.
10. Kosmin and Lachman, ibid, page 14.

CHAPTER 2

1. Roof, ibid, page 132.
2. Greeley, *Andrew, Religious Change in America*, (Cambridge, MA: Harvard University Press, 1989), pages 40–41.
3. Charles Colson, in Colson, Charles and Neuhaus, Richard John, editors, *Evangelicals and Catholics Together*, (Dallas, TX: Word Publishing, 1995), page 38.
4. Richard John Neuhaus, in Colson, Charles and Neuhaus, Richard John,

editors, *Evangelicals and Catholics Together*, (Dallas, TX: Word Publishing, 1995), page 223.

CHAPTER 3
1. Gallup and Castelli, ibid, page 60.
2. Roof, ibid, page 72.
3. Sweeting, George, *Who Said That?*, (Chicago, IL: Moody Press, 1995), page 93.
4. Gallup, George H., Jr. and Poloma, Margaret, *Varieties of Prayer*, (Philadelphia, PA: Trinity Press, 1991), page 125.
5. Wagner, C. Peter, *Your Spiritual Gifts Can Help Your Church Grow*, (Ventura, CA: Regal Books, 1994), page 14.
6. Roof, ibid, page 69.
7. Naisbitt, John and Aburdene, Patricia, *Megatrends 2000*, (New York, NY: William Morrow & Company, 1990), pages 277, 280.
8. Kosmin and Lachman, ibid, page 10.

CHAPTER 4
1. Naisbitt and Aburdene, ibid, page 273.
2. Anderson, ibid, page 34.
3. Bellah et. al., page 219.

CHAPTER 5
1. Gallup and Castelli, ibid, page 88.
2. Gallup and Castelli, ibid, page 45.
3. Anderson, ibid, page 33.
4. Gallup and Castelli, ibid, page 90.
5. Bellah et. al., ibid, pages 227–228.
6. Bellah et. al., ibid, page 232.

CHAPTER 6
1. Gallup and Castelli, ibid, page 60.
2. Bellah et. al., ibid, page 219.
3. Patterson, James and Kim, Peter, *The Day America Told the Truth*, (New York, NY: Prentice Hall Press, 1991), page 199.
4. Gallup and Poloma, ibid, page 16.
5. Wagner, C. Peter, *Churches That Pray*, (Ventura, CA: Regal Books, 1993), pages 17–18.

6. Gallup and Castelli, ibid, page 24.
7. Roof, ibid, page 194.
8. Gallup and Castelli, ibid, page 252.

CHAPTER 7
1. Patterson and Kim, ibid, page 201.

CHAPTER 9
1. Gallup and Castelli, ibid, page 48.
2. Roof, ibid, page 56.
3. Roof, ibid, page 110.
4. Hunter, James Davison, *Culture Wars*, (New York, NY: Basic Books, 1991), pages 76–77.

CHAPTER 10
1. Gallup and Castelli, ibid, page 21.
2. Patterson and Kim, ibid, page 199.
3. Toffler, Alvin, *Power Shift*, (New York, NY: Bantam Books, 1990), pages 375–376.
4. Georgia Anne Geyer, *Washington Post*.
5. Roof, ibid, page 97.
6. Bellah et. al., ibid, page 246.
7. Roof, ibid, page 200.
8. Sweeting, ibid, page 142.
9. Patterson and Kim, ibid, page 200.

CHAPTER 11
1. Bellah et. al., ibid, page 247.

APPENDIX 2

REFERENCES

Anderson, Leith; *A Church for the 21st Century*; Bethany House Publishers, Minneapolis, MN; 1992.

Bellah, Robert, et. al.; *Habits of the Heart*; Harper & Row Publishers, New York, NY; 1985.

Bennett, William; *The Index of Leading Cultural Indicators*; Simon & Schuster, New York, NY; 1994.

Carter, Stephen; *The Culture of Disbelief*; Basic Books, New York, NY; 1993.

Colson, Charles; *The Body*; Word Publishing, Dallas, TX; 1992.

Colson, Charles and Neuhaus, Richard John, editors; *Evangelicals and Catholics Together*; Word Publishing, Dallas, TX; 1995.

Gallup, George H., Jr. and Poloma, Margaret; *Varieties of Prayer*; Trinity Press, Philadelphia, PA; 1991.

Gallup, George H., Jr. and Castelli, Jim; *The People's Religion*; Macmillan Publishing Company, New York, NY; 1989.

Greeley, Andrew; *Religious Change in America*; Harvard University Press, Cambridge, MA; 1989.

Hunter, James Davison; *Culture Wars*; Basic Books, New York, NY; 1991.

Kosmin, Barry and Lachman, Seymour; *One Nation Under God*; Harmony Books, New York, NY; 1993.

Naisbitt, John and Aburdene, Patricia; *Megatrends 2000*; William Morrow & Company, New York, NY; 1990.

Patterson, James and Kim, Peter; *The Day America Told the Truth*; Prentice Hall Press, New York, NY; 1991.

Roof, Wade Clark; *A Generation of Seekers*; Harper Collins, New York, NY; 1993.

Sussman, Barry; *What Americans Really Think*; Pantheon Books, New York, NY; 1988.

Sweeting, George; *Who Said That?*; Moody Press, Chicago, IL; 1995.

Toffler, Alvin; *Power Shift*; Bantam Books, New York, NY; 1990.

Wagner, C. Peter; *Churches That Pray*; Regal Books, Ventura, CA; 1993.

Wagner, C. Peter; *Your Spiritual Gifts Can Help Your Church Grow*; Regal Books, Ventura, CA; 1994.

Yankelovich, Daniel; *New Rules*; Houghton Mifflin, Boston, MA; 1982.

OTHER RESOURCES FROM BARNA RESEARCH RELATED TO AMERICAN SPIRITUALITY

During the past decade, the Barna Research Group has conducted more research on the state of Christianity in America than any other research company. The firm has also collected information regarding other religious faith groups. The following is a listing of some of the resources currently available from Barna Research which discuss trends, conditions, and opportunities related to spirituality.

Related Books by George Barna

Turning Vision into Action, Regal Books, Ventura, CA. 1996

Evangelism That Works. Regal Books, Ventura, CA. 1995.

Generation Next, Regal Books, Ventura, CA. 1995

Turn Around Churches, Regal Books, Ventura, CA. 1993.

The Power of Vision, Regal Books, Ventura, CA. 1992.

Baby Busters, Northfield Publishing, Chicago, IL. 1992.

Today's Pastors, Regal Books, Ventura, CA. 1992.

Search for God, Regal Books, Ventura, CA. 1992.

User Friendly, Churches, Regal Books, Ventura, CA. 1991.

What Americans Believe, Regal Books, Ventura, CA. 1991.

The Frog in the Kettle, Regal Books, Ventura, CA. 1990.

REPORTS

"Raising Money for Ministry," Barna Research Group, Glendale, CA. 1995.

"Casting the Net," Barna Research Group, Glendale, CA. 1995.

"Unmarried America," Barna Research Group, Glendale, CA. 1993.

AUDIOTAPES BY GEORGE BARNA

"Pastoral Leadership Within the Church," produced 1995.

"Understanding Today's Teenagers," produced 1995.

"Effective Evangelism in a Gospel-Resistant Culture," produced 1995.

"How Churches Raise Money for Ministry," produced 1995.

"Creating a User Friendly Church," produced 1992.

VIDEOTAPES

"The Church in a Changing Culture," Word Ministry Resources, Waco, TX. 1994

"Ten Myths About Evangelism," Gospel Light Videos, Ventura, CA. 1995

"Trends That Are Changing Your Ministry World," Gospel Light Videos, Ventura, CA. 1995

"How to Turn Around Your Church," Gospel Light Videos,

Ventura, CA. 1995

"What Evangelistic Churches Do," Gospel Light Videos, Ventura, CA. 1995

"Understanding Today's Teens," Gospel Light Videos, Ventura, CA. 1996

"The Power of Vision," Gospel Light Videos, Ventura, CA. 1996

"Turning Vision Into Action," Gospel Light Videos, Ventura, CA. 1996

"Raising Money for Your Church," Gospel Light Videos, Ventura, CA. 1996

NEWSLETTER (SUBSCRIPTION-BASED)

The Barna Report, Word Ministry Resources, Waco, TX.

BARNA RESEARCH GROUP, LTD.

2487 Ivory Way, Oxnard, CA. 93930